Lipan Chief Castillo – 1854
(Last Days of Chief Castillo – Sun Otter Band)

&

My Ancestral Journey
(Planned Research and Unplanned Occurrences)

Thomas Ruiz Castillo
"Tom BearClaw"

Lipan Nde' of Texas
Corpus Christi, Texas

Castillo, Thomas R.
Lipan Chief Castillo – 1854 / My Ancestral Journey
1st Edition

ISBN: 979-8-218-68928-5   (paperback)

Edited by: Joaquin Rivaya-Martinez PhD
Texas State University

David Gohre PhD
Texas A&M Kingsville

1st Proof: Diana M. Castillo
2nd Proof: Pedro Salinas Flores (Lipan Apache)

Cover Illustrations:
Front Top
"South Texas Lipan Warrior "
Credit: Noe Bazan (Lipan Apache)

Front Bottom
"Nopal Family Tree"
Credit Coral Castillo (Lipan Apache)

Lipan Nde' of Texas
4553 Dandridge Dr
Corpus Christi, TX 78413
Publication Department (361) 215-5121

Dedicated to my immediate family, extended family, and distant relatives. May this be an inspiration to you to continue your family research and to continue, or revive, our Lipan customs, traditions, and ways.

Acknowledgments

We need to recognize some important contributors to this work. All of which had critical input to this historical account.

Bob Apache (Cervantes): Thanks to Bob for his natural insight abilities, intuition and his willingness to share them with me. Also, for the spiritualism that he had graciously offered to me and my family. Bob was a great inspiration for this project and continues to be present in our family's hearts. Bob, Enjoy the Happy Hunting Grounds, I hope to talk with you again someday.

Nancy McGown-Minor: It was undoubtedly an honor to have known you. You inspired my desire to seek, gather and compile the information presented here through your continued quires about the Castillo's. Almost every time we got the opportunity to converse you would ask about the Castillo's history, as if you knew or perhaps felt something of importance was there. Unfortunately, I was not able to share my discoveries with you, for time was not our friend. However, I take comfort in believing that you are aware of this and are pleased with answer to your questions.

Sherry Robinson: I could not have put this project together without your direction and sense of order. Your willingness to provide guidance on structure was invaluable. Thank you for taking time to help on this historical recollection. Also, for your knowledge of the Lipan Apache and eagerness to share it.

Larry Running Turtle Salazar: Thank you my friend for your inspiration and encouragement for me to find my path to my Lipan heritage.

Gary Perez: Thanks for guiding me through the importance of Celestial significance which was, and still is, vital to the Lipan Nde'.

Acknowledgments Con'd

David Gohre: Thanks for your unselfish willingness to always help, and your support for the Lipan Nde'. But most of all your friendship.

Joaquin Rivaya-Martinez: A special thanks for your help and guidance by taking your time to review and edit this project. Also thank you for all you do for the Indigenous Peoples of the Americas.

Pedro Salinas Flores: Your expertise in genealogy and your literary knowledge help with proofing this project is greatly appreciated as well as your enthusiasm to contribute to the Lipan Nde'.

Thanks to others who also contributed to this work:

Thomas Alex - Map

Noe Bazan - Illustration

Coral Castillo - Illustration

Diana M. Castillo - Proofing

Emilio Castillo - Oral History

Andres Gutierrez Camarillo - Photo

Lucille Contreras - Photo

Ruben and Anabeth Cordova - Photo

Pedro Salinas Flores - Proofing

David Gohre - Editing

Diana Moreno - Research & Guidance

Gary Perez - Interview

Lori Podasky - Research & Guidance

Eric Shroder - Research & Guidance

Joaquin Rivaya-Martinez - Editing

Matilda Torres - Research & Guidance

Juan and Malinda Villarreal - Photo

Linda Walking Woman - Reference Guidance

Juliette Wood - Jim Wells County Land Office

To My Family

My Mother, Dorothy Ruiz (Maiden): You kept our family's knowledge of everyday Lipan life alive. Thank you for your reassurance and passing down of these ways even to your last days with us.

My Father, Reyes Castillo: You kept me inspired through your perseverance in life. You taught me that there is strength in silence, as well as the ability to achieve with unfaltering determination.

My Wife, Diana M Castillo: Thank you for always being there and supporting me throughout this endeavor. You have unequivocally stood in support of the indigenous life and have always encouraged our children to not forget their ancestry, either Indigenous or British.

Granet (LongBow), Coral (Morning Star), and Stone Castillo (Silent Hawk): This is for you, my children; your children, and your children's children. This Castillo history was almost lost to time as so much already has. You all have been a great inspiration and motivator for me to continue and persevere with this project. It is my hope that you will continue the legacy of Lipan Chief Castillo, for you are the 7th generation of Chief Castillo.

My Brother, Reyes Castillo Jr: My free-spirited brother, you live your life in need of adventure and freedom. You have the enthusiasm of a true Lipan, never settling down in one place for too long. Wherever you are now, thanks for your Lipan inspiration.

My Sisters, Elvia Lorena and Nieves Castillo (Maiden): Thank you for bearing with me. I know this has been a long time in the making and you have waited patiently. I hope your children will also continue our ancestor's heritage by honoring Chief Castillo's ultimate sacrifice for our people.

All my extended family: I hope this project brings you a sense of inspiration to get more acquainted with our indigenous Lipan heritage, and to keep our Native Identities alive.

And to all those that have inspired me by continuing your Indigenous ways. Thank you to all who have been with me during ceremonies, gatherings, and practice of our cultures and traditional ways.

This page intentionally left blank.

"The United States annexed Texas in 1845 and subjected the state's Native Americans to its national policies of Indian removal, but the Apaches refused to surrender. In response, the U.S. Army increased troop strength at forts on or near Lipan lands, and throughout the 1850's the U.S. Army mounted missions against Lipan encampments." [1]

-Patrick Ryan

-Of military action against the Lipan-

"The war on this frontier is one of extermination.",
Troops were ordered "to take no prisoners", and "to spare no one."

-Brigadier General Albert J. Myer [2]

Part I

Lipan Chief Castillo - 1854

Table of Contents:
Part I
Lipan Chief Castillo – 1854

Table of Contents cont'd

Lipan Chief Castillo – 1854 / My Ancestral Journey

Citations and Credits:

Lipan Chief Castillo 1854

Introduction

Since the inception of the United States of America in 1776 the peoples indigenous to this country have not been welcomed on their own land, and in fact have been victims of domicide. This is evident in the document that helped to initiate the United States of America: The Declaration of Independence. Within this document it was made clear that this "Independence" was fostered for the "European White Americans". The wording of this document included, "…the merciless Indian savages…", which for all intents and purposes, and in and of itself, serves to exclude the Indigenous peoples as part of the "Declared Independent". It also serves to indicate that the Indigenous peoples were not accepted as part of the "…all men are created equal…" in this document. (As well as the Black people in America by virtue of their slavery.)

By 1845 this "idea" of the European White American was still in existence and expanding westward into the new frontier. The philosophy pronounced by the ideology of the "Manifest Destiny", which expressed the need to get rid of the indigenous, is that the "European White Americans" could successfully conquer the west. Further strengthening the resolve of the European White Americans was the 1830 Indian Removal Act, which led to the ethnic cleansing of the land east of the Mississippi. This continued the systematic elimination of Indigenous human rights, circumvented basic political, economic, and cultural identities, by way of killings, displacement and forced assimilation to decimate the Indigenous

5

peoples within the borders of the United States of America. These threats are faced by the indigenous peoples of the United States of American even today.

All Tribal Nations have been affected by this European White American desire to own, and profit off the lands which were used by the indigenous peoples for their livelihood. The Apache peoples were spared no sympathy for their part. The United States of America pursued the Apache People and fought many a battle, and scuffles, in their attempt to subdue these proud peoples. Battles such as the Battle at Fort Apache, September 1, 1881 (White Mountain Apache), Victorio's War, September 4, 1879 - October 1880 (Warm Springs and Mescalero Apache), Battle of Cieneguilla, March 30, 1854 (Jicarilla Apache), Battle of Apache Pass, July 15-16, 1862 (Chiricahua Apache), were among the most famous for the Apache. The Lipan Apache also had their share of battle engagements. Still, most of the more notable were in coalition with other militia such as in the Battle of Medina, August 18, 1813, as they sided with the insurgent forces, the Battle of Salado Creek, September 17, 1842, again fighting along side Tejano forces. The Lipan did have some battles independent of allies. One was the Battle of Diablo Mountains vs. U.S. Army, October 3, 1854 and Skirmish on Live Oak Creek vs. Comanche, July or August, 1840, . Missing from the pages of most historical accounts however is a Lipan Battle that led to the killing of a Lipan Chief, Castillo. Due to a false accusation, and the U.S. apparently needing an excuse to justify the eradication of a Lipan Clan [3], Castillo paid the ultimate price for his people.

The United States has continued to use false accusations as means to justify war on several occasions. For instance, the USS Maine

Disaster, February 15, 1898, the Spanish-American War, April 21, 1898 - December 10, 1898, World War II, September1, 1939 - September 2, 1945, Vietnam, November 1, 1955 - April 30, 1975 and the 1st Gulf War, August 2, 1990 - February 28, 1991. The use of this scheme even led to the Executive Accountability Act of 2009, which prohibited the executive branch of government from knowingly and willfully falsifying information to mislead congress in order to secure authorization for the use of the military forces.

Using these same tactics the United States of America attempted to deal with the Apache, in particular the Lipan Apache. However it did not manage to eradicate or exterminate us.

Today the Lipan Apache of Texas are coming together and are reclaiming their heritage, culture, and traditions. Two main groups are bringing the Lipan Apache of Texas together, The Lipan Apache Band of Texas and The Lipan Apache Tribe of Texas. There is also a group that deals with the traditional, social and cultural aspects of the Lipan Apache, The Lipan Nde' of Texas.

Preface

The inspiration for this, part I, came when I realized that documented history lacked a cohesive account of the last days of my ancestor Lipan Chief Castillo. I feel there is also an absence of the importance associated with the events that unfolded in 1854 concerning the last remnants of the Sun Otter Band of South Texas.

The nineteenth century saw a big change in the lifestyle and ferocity of the Lipan Nde'. To borrow a phrase used for the month of March, "It came in like a lion, and ended like a lamb."

This book is about a particular victimization and attacks on one Lipan clan and its Chief, Lipan Chief Castillo, by the U.S. Army in the spring and summer of 1854.

It is important to note that Lipan spiritualism quite possibly had a big impact on the final days of Lipan Chief Castillo. Not only did the Lipan turn to Peyote and their celestial knowledge for guidance in healing, but also for, political and warfare conveyance.[4] This Celestial/Peyote spiritualism will be acknowledged in this project; nonetheless, the details will not be made available as they are sacred, and it would be inappropriate to have them be divulged here. I can nevertheless reveal that the Peyote Ceremony dates back further than most historians argue. This spiritualism plays an important role in the historical events as they unfold.

Still, through the immense strife, Lipans managed to counter, thanks to our perseverance, spiritualism, and pride. However, when the dust of conflict was settling, some Lipan yielded to the Spanish Missions,[5] some resorted to life on a reservation,[6] others moved away to Mexico and others tried to avoid persecution and discrimination by assimilating into the local population[7] by suppressing or hiding most of our indigenous customs, traditions and unfortunately, even the

8

language. But, through it all, there still remained those unwavering Lipans that would not give up their way of life and would rather fight till the end.[8] Lipans were being scattered like smoke in the wind throughout the 1850's.

According to Thomas A Britten, (The Lipan Apaches, 2009). "Facing starvation, frequent and involuntary relocations, declining trade opportunities, and sporadic but deadly clashes with soldiers, the Lipan Apaches of the 1850's were in the most desperate position in their history-they were, in essence, teetering on the brink of extinction." I would like to add that it would be an extinction of a Tribe, but not its people.

1854, in particular, was a very busy and consequential year for the Lipan. Especially where warfare was involved. Lipans were in a struggle for our mere existence. That year engulfed the Lipan in numerous skirmishes and battles. In the most notable one, the Battle of Diablo Mountains, October 3, 1854 the U.S. Army attacked a Lipan camp.

Since several U.S. Army Forts will be mentioned throughout this work let us take a minute to familiarize you with their locations. **Fort Merrill**: Was at near present-day Dinero, Texas, in Live Oak County on present-day Lake Corpus Christi. **Fort Ewell**: Was near present-day Cotulla, Texas in La Salle County at the intersection of the Nueces River and present-day Highway I-35. **Fort Inge**: Is at present-day Uvalde, Texas in Uvalde County and is about 1 mile from the city. **Fort McIntosh**: Was at present-day Laredo, Texas in Webb County. **Army Headquarters for Texas at Camp Corpus Christi**: Was at present-day Corpus Christi, Texas in Nueces County.
[Map 1 South Texas Forts in 1854 pg. 10]

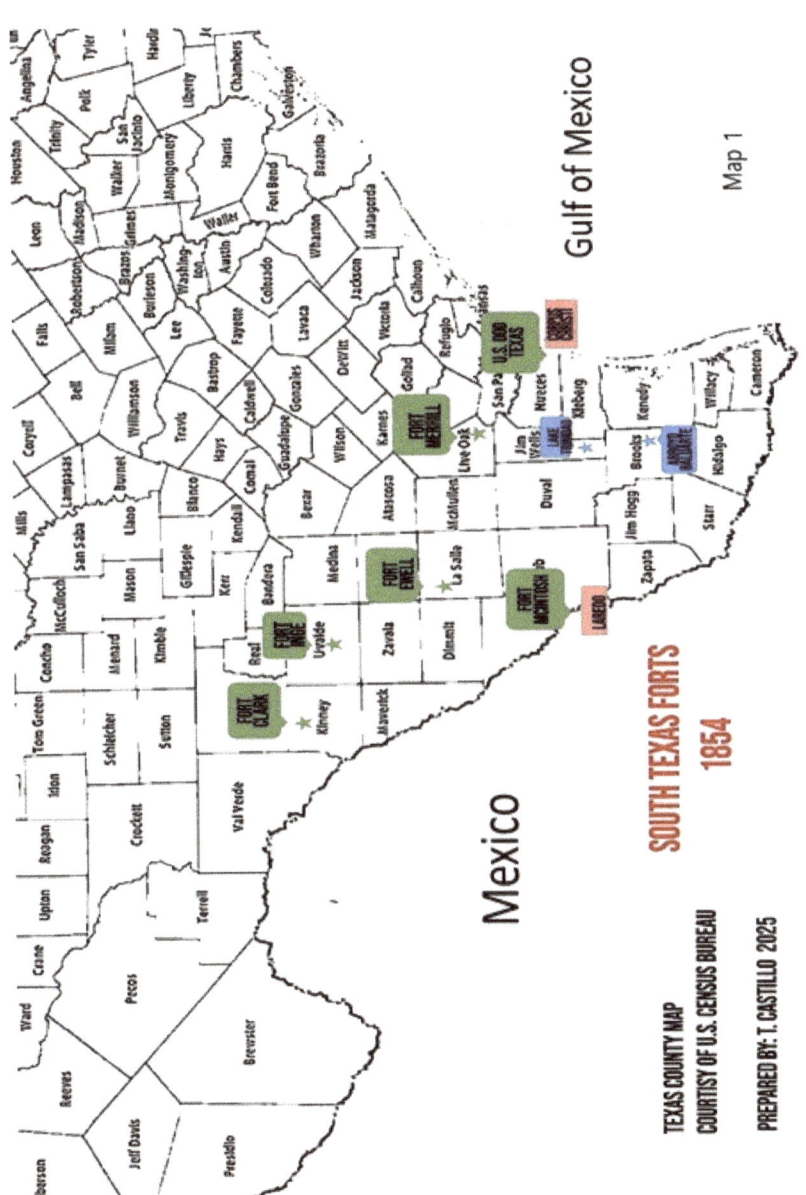

SOUTH TEXAS FORTS
1854

TEXAS COUNTY MAP
COURTISY OF U.S. CENSUS BUREAU

PREPARED BY: T. CASTILLO 2025

Gulf of Mexico

Map 1

Mexico

Chapter 1
Lipan Apache Lifestyle in the 1850's

In the early days of 1854, the weather in South Texas would have been as any other winter. Temperatures ranged from the Mid-40's to Mid-60's with possibly 1-1/2 inches of precipitation. This would have led to the gearing up for work that was soon needed. Preparations for planting would have begun in February just prior to, or following, the last frosts and lasted possibly into March. The Lipan have been noted as planters of corn, squash, and beans among other food sources.[9] Our people would also forage wild plants such as prickly pear cactus and its tuna, wild onion, mesquite beans, pecans, persimmon, and pawpaw to name a few.[10,11] Preparing the soil, planting crops, and gathering food kept the Lipan people busy everyday. [12,13]

Hunting was also very important to the Lipan. It provided a necessary form of protein, a sense of pride through the hunt, and helped to establish one as a warrior, by demonstrating his ability to skillfully use a bow and arrow and a lance, for the people.[14] The hunt during that period of time would have been accompanied by several forms of tools for the hunt including, tracking skills[15], making and using bow and arrows, spears, and knowledge of trapping skills. Having good horsemanship was also a plus. The game available in South Texas in 1854 consisted usually of medium to small game. The deer, javelins, feral hogs, wild turkey were the prized catch. Also, on the menu was smaller game such as, squirrel, opossum, rabbit, armadillo, and quail.[16] During dire periods the Lipan also pandered in insects, snakes, lizards, and fish. These were of very last resort since for instance fish lived in water which is a sacred element to the Apache. Also, it is taboo to eat reptiles or any animal with scales. Due to over hunting and drought conditions the once important food staple, the bison, was on its rapid decline and in 1854 it was getting harder and harder to rely on them as a food and tool source. [17,18,19,20] [picture 1 American Bison In Texas – pg.13] The depletion of the bison meant that the coverings for the Lipan Teepee would have to change. The Lipans would begin to use Teepee covers made of canvas which they procured via the U.S. Government.[21]

With venison as a highly sought after prize for food, so were its hides for making clothes during the beginning of the 1800's. The typical style of cloth was morphing from buckskin to cotton as the latter was becoming more popular as a trade item. By the 1850's it was apparent that the style of clothes was evolving.
[pictures 2a Buckskin Clothing. 2b Lipan Cotton Clothing– pg.14] Cloth and clothes trade (not to leave out the ware that was taken via raids) was evident by the styles the Lipan were now evolving to either by design (wanting to be in style) or by necessity (buckskin can be heavy and hot for the typical South Texas weather). The weather played a major factor, using cotton for most of the year and buckskin during winter months.[22] Blankets also played a big part of the Lipan style as they were worn year-round, (for cool spring, summer and fall nights) and during the winter and ceremonies. [23] Clothing was very important to Lipan, especially having to deal with the arid climate and the harsh conditions of the South Texas chaparral.

[Picture 1] **American Bison in Texas** – Courtesy of Lucille Contreras and the **Texas Tribal Buffalo Project**. Waelder, Texas (Gonzales County)

[Picture 3 **South Texas Chaparral**
Courtesy of The Red Sun Ranch
(Juan & Melinda Villarreal)

[Picture 2a] **Buckskin Clothing**
Source: Berlanier (1828) "The Indians of Texas in 1830"
 (Open Domain)
Credit: Watercolor by - Lino Sanchez y Tapia after Jose Maria
Sanchez Y Tapia

[Picture 2b] **Cotton Clothing** – Still used today.
Source Credit: Courtesy of Anabeth and Ruben Cordova
 (2012 McAllen, Texas)

The natural South Texas terrain mostly consisted of thorny shrubs, mesquite, acacia (Huisache), prickly pear cactus, and Yucca, to name a few. [picture 3 South Texas Chaparral – pg.13] The terrain was mostly arid throughout the region but there was enough water to sustain the flora, fauna, and indigenous peoples. Water would be available primarily through a few rivers, the Nueces, Rio Grande, San Antonio, and Guadalupe. However, there were plenty of other sources from seasonal arroyos, creeks, and small lakes. [map 2 Texas Rivers - pg.17] The land also provided the Lipan with some very important spiritual provisions such as Peyote, cattail pollen, colored ochre, Texas sage, and cedar to mention a few. This terrain help sustain Lipans for hundreds of years.

The Apache first appeared in Texas around 1530's and slowly made their way to South Texas by the 1600's and managed to survive.[24,25] Helping to endure life in South Texas was the close family ties the Lipan had, as with most peoples around the world, a strong family support group would help to ensure survival. The Lipan consisted of groups of various sizes. Most family groups (immediate and extended) had "Headmen", that the families would turn to for advice and leadership at a rancheria. These headmen groups would be considered a "clan" with a collection of the clans, headed by a "Jefe" (Chief) belonging to a band, the collect of all the bands was considered the tribe.[26] There was no "centralized" Leadership for the Tribe, however the U.S. tried to negotiate with some overall Head Chief as to represent the Tribe as a whole. The U.S. soon found out that Chiefs represented clans and bands and did not adhere to the dealing of some of the other Chiefs if they felt it was not appropriate for their group(s) as the Spanish had encountered over a century prior. [27,28,29]

Castillo's clan was embedded in an area at or near Agua Dulce, Texas in what is today, Nueces County, East of Alice, Texas, a small community which had recently at the time been established. The camp was located off of what is today Highway 44 between Alice, Texas and Corpus Christi, Texas [map 3 South Texas Towns – pg.18]. Castillo's clan can be estimated using the number of warriors he led, ~40.[30] Therefor it is safe to say that Castillo's group consisted of about 30-40 families, with about 40 men (warriors), 40 women (of working age) and 80 children and elders. That would put the group, as a whole, at 160 individuals. [31,32] Even though Lipan Chiefs at times took in more than one wife, Chief Castillo himself had at least 1 wife [33,34] and at least 1 child.[35]

The Lipan Apache of Texas lived a particular lifestyle that evolved throughout hundreds of years. This lifestyle encompassed using what nature offered in the specific area that they traversed into and out of.

Lipan Chief Castillo - 1854

Source: GISGeography.com

Map 2

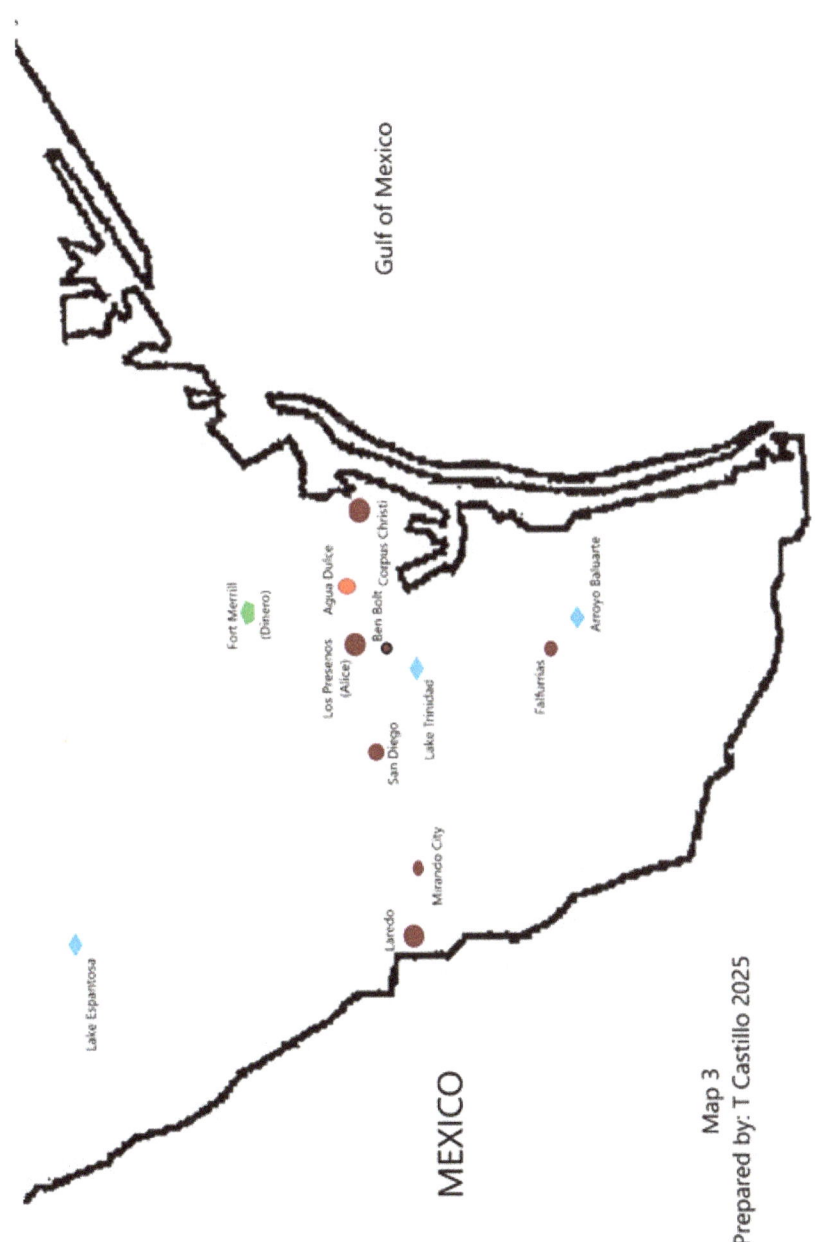

Gulf of Mexico

Fort Merrill
(Dinero)

Agua Dulce

Ben Bolt · Corpus Christi

Los Presenos
(Alice)

Lake Trinidad

San Diego

Falfurrias

Arroyo Baluarte

Mirando City

Laredo

Lake Espantosa

MEXICO

Map 3
Prepared by: T Castillo 2025

Chapter 2
It Begins

      January and February of 1854 saw an exceptionally large amounts of Indian depredations around the Laredo, Texas area, its vicinity, and nearby ranches. Too much the displeasure of the local citizens and ranchers, the Lipan Apache had lived and traveled in this area for many decades if not centuries. The Lipan had a bad reputation as far the "civilized citizens" were concerned. It would seem that these citizens and ranchers would like nothing more than to rid the area of these savage Lipan from their own lands.[36] This combined with the numerous "Indian problems" would be the cause for false accusations against the Lipan Apache.[37] It will become apparent, that this led to actions against the Lipan.

      Throughout these two months there were reports of several incidents that implicated "Indians': from general depredations to thief of horses, cattle, and pigs, and destruction of property.[38] To make matters worse there was also the killing of several citizens throughout this two-month ordeal. It was recorded that there were up to 7 casualties, including that of Don Crisento Bela a well-known and widely respected citizen of the area.[39,40] What didn't help the situations, and brought even more distraught to the local citizens, was the fact that in most occasions the perpetrators were able to get away scott-free.

      The U.S. Army was not able to assist in a timely manner to these incidents because the Army Post which served the Laredo area (Fort McIntosh) would be informed too late to engage and was left to only track the culprits. The "Indians" knew that they could cause their harm and get away quickly since that had occurred in several assaults, and so they persisted.[41] Fort McIntosh was also not equipped with enough military provisions to offer relief to the citizens, even if they cared to. [42] Fort McIntosh also lacked the proper capability to offer a pursue and attack strategy since at the time it consisted of 500 soldiers and no mounted attachment.[43] It would seem the only defense the Citizens of Laredo and the surrounding area had was the sounding of church bells. [44]

The Citizens needed to bring a stop to these attacks and needed to point the finger to someone so as to possibly obtain some sort of extra assistance from either the U.S. Government or the State of Texas. It would seem that the Lipan could be used as a scapegoat by the local citizens, to be rid of Lipans, and in hopes to ease in the troubles of late. The Lipan Apache were blamed for much of, if not all, of the problematic events that were taking place. [45] The Citizens apparently produced a eyewitness who they insisted could identify the raiders as Lipan Apache since he said he (Trinidad Ramos) had met and knew some of the members of the Lipan group. [46] But the "Lipan" he knew and recognized which he alleged to be the culprits were in fact members of "Chief Chepota's" group at Fort Inge. [47] Chief Chepota's group, at Fort Inge, were a Band of the Lipan de Arriba division of Lipan, which will turn out to be an important detail later on.

In the beginning of the 1850's quite a few depredations were accruing in and around the Laredo area. Locals pointed fingers at the Lipan Apache which frequented the area on occasion, however without merit. It would seem that these citizens had an ulterior motive, to rid the area of the Lipan Apache.

Chapter 3
<u>Peyote and Spiritualism</u>

It is important to veer away from the published, printed, recorded, or otherwise documented aspect of this project and refer to the Peyote Ceremonies and Spiritualism. This facet of Lipan life is for the most part a very sacred issue that has throughout the ages been kept by the Lipan as such, and there for, details will not be divulged. It is, however, important to understand that these customs had an effect on the decisions and outcomes of Lipan peoples. I can disclose some things without too much repercussion only because is important for the understanding of this project.[48,49] This is well documented, that the Lipan have used Spiritualism and Ceremonies to petition help with political, weather, war, hunting, health, prosperity, and other aspects of life. Most, if not all, publications to date refer to ceremony and spiritualism among the Lipan as a generality, referring just to the mechanical aspects of the ceremony.[50] What has not been made public is the "Why", in particular, why things are done the way they are. I will say that for the most part all aspects of ceremonies are done with particular reason, including the Peyote ceremony.

The Peyote ceremony is where I run into a slippery slope. It has been inferred by some researchers that the ceremony originated with the Lipans as a means to heal the sick and gotten from the Carrizo's.[51] This could have been an avenue in which some Lipans may have acquired the use of Peyote for ceremony, and that is widely used and accepted since it was "passed" along to and from other Indigenous

Peoples. There is yet another channel that may, or may not have been, part of these passed on ceremonies which eventually ended up with the NAC (Native American Church). This ancient way entrenched in the original Lipan Peyote ceremony encompasses the interrelationship of, time, cosmos, geography, flora, and fauna as well as other aspects which are depicted in man-made symbolism. This involves a very complex and complicated system. Due to the delicate nature and sophistication of these ways it is beyond the scope of this project. Further divergence into this Ancestral Lipan Peyote Ceremony will be examined in a forthcoming separate project. The purpose here is just to vaguely familiarize you with the possibility for reasoning behind some activities and decisions made by the Lipan and the U.S. Army.

Using the knowledge of these ancestral ways it is reasonable to determine that in the beginning of March 1854 Chief Castillo and some of his group were at the Peyote gardens of South Texas either to prepare for ceremony or harvesting peyote. They would have traveled from South of "Presenos" (Los Preseños, then became Collins), Texas which now is current day Alice, Texas[52,53,54] near Lake Trinidad (Just south of what is today Ben Bolt, Texas right off of highway 281 in Jim Wells County) and almost due East-Southeast to these gardens near Mirando City.[55]
[map 4 Traveled Directions – pg.24] Which would be 30 mi. or less from Laredo, Texas. Castillo's group would have stayed a couple or maybe three days before returning home.
Upon the return the tracks left would have led westward back to near Lake Trinidad. Also, it is important to note that Chief Castillo's group were Lipan de Abajo.[56]

A critical aspect of the Lipan lifestyle to many of their people was the practice of using peyote in ceremony. Most of the intricacies of these ceremonies have been kept within a few of the Lipan people. This is partly due to the ceremony, as we will see, being used as an instrument against Lipans.

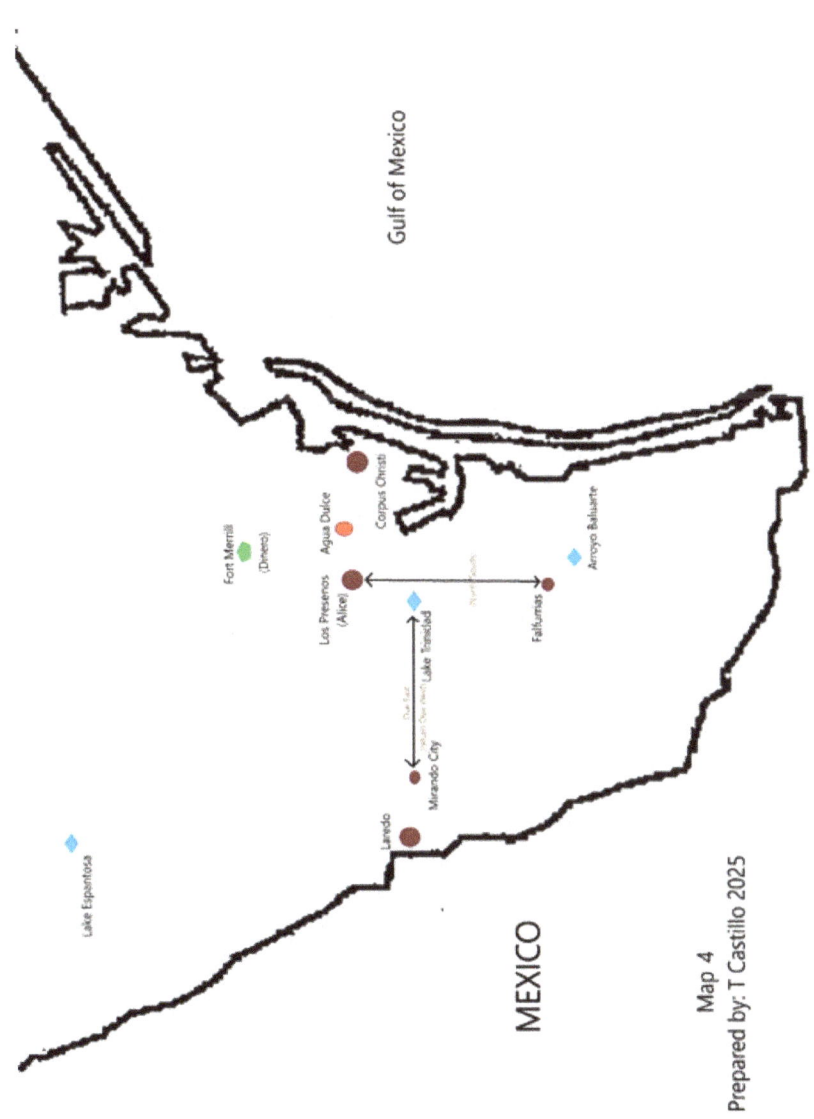

Gulf of Mexico

Fort Merrill
(Dinero)

Corpus Christi

Agua Dulce

Los Presenos
(Alice)

Falfurrias

Arroyo Baluarte

Lake Trinidad

Mirando City

Laredo

Lake Espantosa

MEXICO

Map 4
Prepared by: T Castillo 2025

Chapter 4
Frustrations Set In

On March 9th, 1854, at mid-day Indians attacked a Mexican wagon train near Laredo, Texas that was headed towards H.P. Bee's ranch and eventually that afternoon some citizens arrived to help and ran off the Indians.[57] According to reports some Mexicans were injured, and some ran away into the brush to hide. Sometime later, possibly the next morning, a detachment which had just returned from a scouting expedition set out to find the perpetrators. Led by Lieutenant Witter from Fort McIntosh, the detachment went in search of a trail. They picked up a trail and pursued it for approximately fifty-five miles until, according to Lieutenant Witter, they lost it "in the mountains".[58]

It is important to point out that there is a big discrepancy here since there are no mountains within 100 miles of Laredo, Texas. The topography is relatively flat within a fifty-five-mile radius of the city. [map 5 Topographical Map Laredo, Texas Area – pg.29] There are, however, tall plateaus with deep arroyos throughout the peyote gardens, which are within the fifty-five-mile range. It is a good possibility that this could have been the place referred to by Lieutenant Witter where "the trail was lost." To get to that location, the detachment would have been traveling due **east**, in the direction of Chief Castillo's camp.

H.P. Bee and his family were so distraught from this ordeal that they abandoned the ranch and proceeded to live within the confines of the city of Laredo.[59] The citizens of Laredo proceeded to blame Lipans as the culprits of the incident. In particular they blamed the Lipan that were in Fort Inge (members of Chief Chipota's group) as being responsible for the event,[60] please keep in mind that Fort Inge is due north of Laredo, Texas as a crow flies.

By now the citizens of Laredo and the surrounding area and ranches were fed-up with the multitude of Indian raids and degeneracies from the occurrences which happened in January and February, and now, this Mexican train incident was, in a matter of speaking, the last straw. The citizens and ranchers were now demanding that something be done on their behalf to receive some sort of relief that they felt was owed to them.

Chapter 5
Notice Given

The citizens of Laredo and the local ranchers were now at wits end. They wanted their collective voices heard. On March 11th two days after the Mexican wagon train incident the citizens of Laredo and surrounding ranches met to discuss a solution for this problem of intrusion and deprivation.[61] The meeting was held at the Court House in Laredo. Two of the dignitaries at the citizens' meeting were E.J. Davis who was called to Chair the meeting and Tomas Travenio, named Secretary. A committee was formed after discussion and explanations, appointed to the committee to prepare a report and resolution resulting of the meeting were as follows: H.P. Bee, Jose M. Gonzales (Chair), Agustin Soto, Bentura Gonzales, Alvino Trevino, Eugenio Garza, and J.A. Wilkinson.[62]

The report included the incidents, the loss of lives, the loss of property, the local Fort's (McIntosh) inability to protect due to, lack of proper equipment, capability and lack of readiness of personnel, and/or incapability to pursue the Indians. The report further stated that the U.S. Government was responsible for the protection and upkeep of peace in its territory. Yet that the citizens and surrounding ranches were not being serviced even though they paid their taxes, and further, the heavy duties imposed upon them by the U.S. Government when they needed to purchase crop goods from Mexico due the depletion's of their crops by the raiding Indians.[63] It went on to say that the State of Texas would send Rangers at the cost of the citizens and ranchers but only a few could afford the contracts, nor did they want the Rangers, believing that it was not their place to deal with these situations.[64] The report included accusations as well. It stated that the citizens believed the problems were orchestrated by the Lipan Indians. Here they named a witness, Trinidad Ramos, that would be willing to testify that the offenders were Lipan Indians, because he claimed he knew some Lipan Indians in Chief Chepita's group.[65]

It is important to note that the report stated that Trinidad Ramos would testify, however there is no evidence that he ever spoke under oath. The citizens and committee used this "testimony" to resolve that they should be allowed to protect themselves and to that end go after the Lipan and even have the authorization for the "...destruction of the whole Tribe."[66] This resolution included the recruitment of men from the Counties of Bexar, Nueces, Star, Hidalgo and Cameron to gather a force of not less than 200 men, to go after "these tamed pets of the U.S." It was further resolved, with an appeal to the U.S. Government, that it should send a significant mounted force to patrol the area as it is a privilege of the citizens.[67] The report and resolutions were sent out to the U.S. Government and the State of Texas on March 13, 1854.[68]

The day after the citizens meeting (March 12, 1854) another incident occurred involving Indians and this was included in the report as well. This event involved the taking of 20 horses and "herds of cattle" from local ranchers.[69,70] Again, the Lipan, as before, were blamed for the affair attributed to the Trinidad Ramos testament. Further enraging the citizens was the inability, once again, to stop or pursue the Indians in question, which led to them getting away.[71]

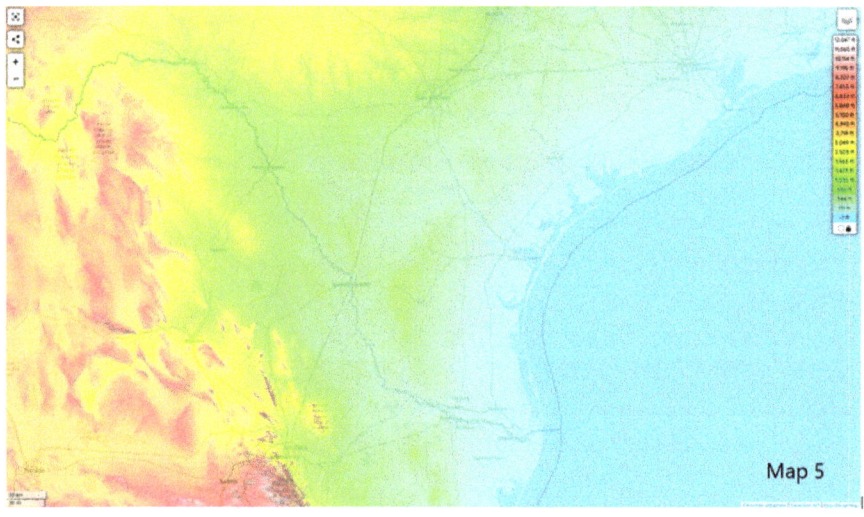

Map 5

There are no "mountains" near Laredo, TX. Much less 45 miles away. Nearest high hills are to the south-east into Mexico and they are only approx., 5000ft. A Mountain is considered a "Mountain" if it is over 8000ft.

Source: https://en-us.topographic-map.com/map-c76tp/Laredo/?center=27.79049%2C-98.5199&zoom=8

Chapter 6

Questionable Allegations

Sometime after the latest incident Lieutenant Witte from Fort McIntosh, with a few of his troops, made an attempt to find the Indians involved in the raid. His attempt though, to locate the trail of the Indians, was unsuccessful. He then proceeded North to Fort Inge where the accused were known to be. [72] Upon arrival at Fort Inge Lieutenant Witte immediately questioned Lipan Chief Chepota concerning the depredations at Laredo. Chief Chepota denied that any of his men were involved in any of the occurrences around the Laredo area. Further stating that Trinidad Ramos does in fact know some of his men. Chief Chepota added that if the raiders were Lipan, it could have been some other group.[73]

The U. S. Indian Agent, Robert S. Neighbors, in charge of the Texas area, was not convinced that the blame should be on Lipans for the problems on the Rio Grande.[74] Texas Governor E. M. Pease also noted in a letter to U. S. Army Major General Persifor F. Smith that at the same time period of the Laredo incidents there were also depredations occurring south of Webb County along the Rio Grande. This would help later to identify who the culprits were that were wreaking havoc along the Rio Grande including the Laredo area.[75] Eventually Agent Neighbors reported on an investigation in the field made by Agent Howard who ascertained that none of the Indians in his charge, which included the Lipan, had been involved in the attacks near Laredo.[76] After further investigation it was found that the perpetrators of the events which had occurred in the Laredo and surrounding areas were actually, and without a bout, the doings of the Northern Comanche and the Wichita Indians![77] "The Lipan contended that the Comanche raiders from the north were responsible. Nevertheless, they were blamed, attacked and "were hence-forth ranked as outlaws, to be shot down at will.""

None the less, General Smith seemed to want retribution from the Lipan for the events in Laredo and the surrounding areas. For whatever reason, needing to satisfy the citizens in Laredo who had demanded U.S. involvement with capture/killing of the Lipan, not wanting to have unresolved problems under his watch, or following U.S. Policies toward Indians at the time, he needed to show some kind of "justice".[78] This mindset of General Smith became very clear when he stated later that the Indians had provided him "an excuse" to begin launching marauding raids against the them.[79]

A good possibility that General Smith's aggregation of frustrations led towards his disdain of the Lipan. That coupled with the fact that many incidents had gone unresolved due to the Army's inability to deal with the Indians under his command could have also added to his frustrations. It was noted time and time again that there was not enough proper equipment, a lack of ammo, lack of horses, lack of troops, and lack of properly trained soldiers to handle the situations then occurring.[80,81] These inadequate preparations seemed to plague Fort McIntosh, Fort Ewell and Fort Merrill who were the Army's "Front Line" for this area. Further adding to General Smiths aggravations was the fact that the U.S. Army was sending troops to the north to handle Indian hostilities on the Oregon Trail and not to Texas. [82]

With General Smith's current view of Lipans as the menace of his irritations, it didn't help his view when, yet two more incidents occurred, and the Lipan were again put to blame. In April 1854 just north of San Antonio, a man named Forrester and his three young daughters were attacked and murdered in their home by three men. It was later found that the actual assailants were the Wichitas.[83] Also happening in April 1854 was the kidnapping of two men west of San Antonio at the Gallagher-Callaghan ranch, again blame fell on Lipans. And yet again it was later discovered that the Lipan were not the perpetrators, it was the Comanche.[84]

Knowing the geographic locations of the two distinct Lipan Apache Tribal divisions Lipans de Arriba (Upper Lipan) and Lipans de Abajo (Lower Lipan) is pertinant to the understanding of false alligations. [map 6 – pg.] Chief Chipota (Uplanders Band) and his group who were originaly "idendified" as the perpretrators and then found not to be, were Lipan de Arriba. Chief Castillo (Sun Otter Band) and his group were Lipan de Abajo, nontheless they were made the target of General Smith.[85] The inability to swiftly identify the culprits of deprdations, lack of nessacery reddiness, and the U.S. Army's incapacity to capture any of the offenders under General Smith's Command led to injustices toward the Lipan Apache of Chief Castillo.

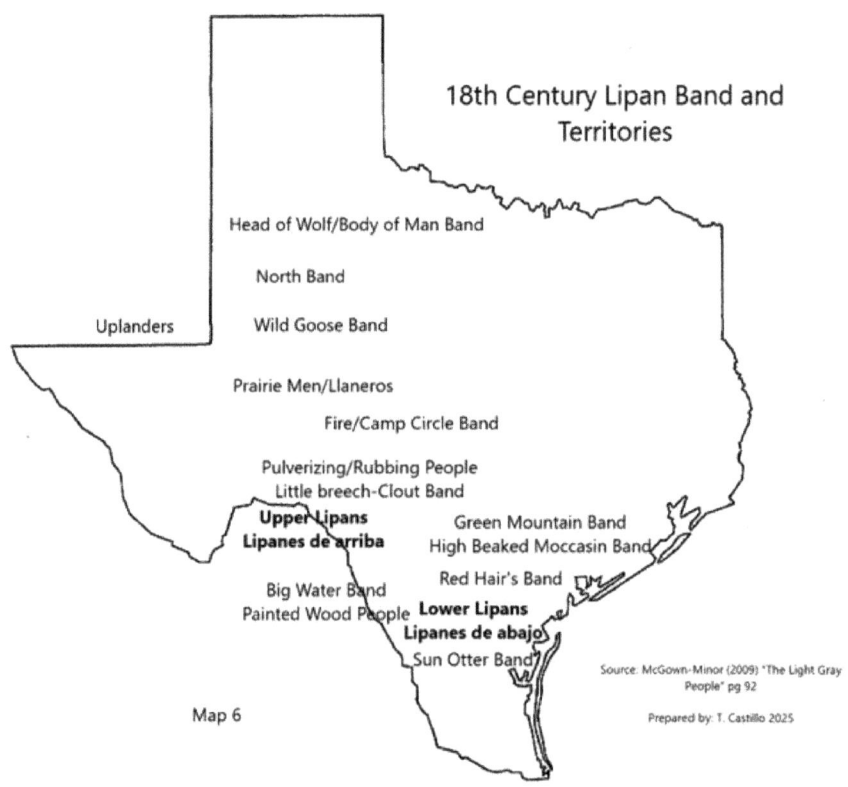

18th Century Lipan Band and
Territories

Head of Wolf/Body of Man Band

North Band

Uplanders   Wild Goose Band

Prairie Men/Llaneros

Fire/Camp Circle Band

Pulverizing/Rubbing People
Little breech-Clout Band
Upper Lipans   Green Mountain Band
Lipanes de arriba   High Beaked Moccasin Band

Red Hair's Band

Big Water Band
Painted Wood People **Lower Lipans**
Lipanes de abajo

Sun Otter Band

Source: McGown-Minor (2009) "The Light Gray
People" pg 92

Map 6   Prepared by: T. Castillo 2025

Chapter 7

Smith Takes Action

Lingering false accusations against Lipans, and the U.S. Army's inability to stop the Indian depredations, mounted a need to save face with the citizens of Laredo and the surrounding area, which then became the catalyst for military actions against the Lipan....any Lipan. General Smith's tolerance for the Lipan had come to an end with another incident that ensued in late April 1854. A train (wagon train) was raided, and 5 men were killed in the attack. The incident occurred just 12 miles from Fort Ewell. Reports do indicate that even though most, if not all, of the Lipans were at Fort Inge at the time of the incident, and had viable alibis, the Texans had convinced themselves that it was Lipans who were at fault and continued long after.[86,87] In that same month General Smith again reiterated his charge against the Lipan and laid blame on the U.S. Indian Services for it. Smith then expressed the U.S. policies to militarily expel Indians from their homelands.[88] Interestingly enough these fake incurable allegations remained long onto the 20th century and still obliging false justice. Even until the date Oct. 11, 2016, the Lipan were still falsely accused of this event as is evident in an Article in the *Corpus Christi Caller-Times*.[89]

"Battle at Lake Trinidad-
In 1854 a wagon train carrying army supplies was attacked by **Lipan Apache** *warriors. Patrols were dispatched from every fort in the region, including Fort Merrill, 50 miles above Corpus Christi..."*

But, as noted earlier, the blame was later found to be squarely on the Comanche and Wichita. And again, this allegation against the Lipan was enough "excuse" for General Smith to initiate military action against Lipans.

At this point, it was apparent that, "some" Lipan group needed to be "made an example of." Since the Headquarters of the Army for Texas was in Corpus Christi at the time, it would seem viable that the U.S. Army was informed as to the whereabouts of Lipan encampments in the area. The U.S. Army during the 1850's did not have a Central Intelligence Division. Each Fort and outpost sent off two types of intelligence gathering. One was routine scouting and reconnaissance, and the other were reports by engineers doing topographical and land surveying who would revel any and all contact and movement of Native Americans they encountered.[90] Even with this intelligence The U.S. Army's assessment of Chief Castillo's group was off the mark, again sending a unit that was unprepared and mal-equipped to conduct an attack. General Smith proceeded to order five detachments of rifle units from Fort Merrill, under the command of Lieutenant G. Cosby to "hunt down the raiders." [91] It is now obvious that the Army knew that Lipan Chief Castillo was in the vicinity. Evidence of this is a report, dated May 10, 1854, from Headquarters Department of Texas, Corpus Christi from Bet. Maj. Gen. Persifor F. Smith.[92]

The report stated that on Monday May 8th, 1854, the Rifle unit from Fort Merrill, under the guidance of Lieutenant Cosby, headed south to Lake Trinidad with about 12 mounted soldiers. [93,94] Here let's take a moment to reflect that the wagon train raid happened to the **west** of Fort Merrill **near** Fort Ewell. Yet, to reiterate General Smith ordered the rifle unit from Fort Merrill to go **south** towards Lake Trinidad. [map 7 Direction of U.S. Army Travel– pg.45] The Army's logic and no preparedness, (as had been the case as of late), for this battle to ensue seem to contradict reason. The Unit sent from Fort Merrill under Cosby's command was allegedly a "Mounted Rifle Unit", yet in the accounts of the battle it is stated that the unit didn't have any rifles. It was reported that the unit only had side arm pistols and little working ammunition for the pistols. [95,96] With the premise of the accusations and the need to avoid humiliation General Smith managed to achieve the opposite by sending an inadequate Unit in an attempt to forcefully procure Chief Castillo's group.

Chapter 8

Lipan Victory – 1ˢᵗ Battle at Lake Trinidad

Lieutenant Cosby, who was sent to attack the Lipans, reaches Lake Trinidad, not finding Lipan Chief Castillo, or his group, the Lieutenant splits up his unit, one lead by a Corporal who took some of the soldiers south in search of Lipans. The other unit, with about 8 mounted soldiers, went with Lieutenant Cosby west towards Santa Gertrudis to find ammunition. Lieutenant Cosby's group having traveled less than a mile was approached by a Mexican who informs Lieutenant Cosby that Castillo's Lipan group arrived at Lake Trinidad after they had left. Lieutenant Cosby immediately returns with his men to Lake Trinidad and locates Lipan Chief Castillo and his group of about 35-40 warriors at the lake.[97]

Similar to General George Armstrong Custer's terrible decision at the Battle of Little Bighorn which ended with his demise, Lieutenant Cosby orders an immediate attack, knowing that they were outnumbered, had no rifles, had only pistols, which were inoperable with no or bad ammunition, and basically only some swords (sabers) to fight with.[98]

According to Corporal William Wright's account, (Through an eyewitness testimony, as he was one of the Mounted Rifle Units' soldiers.), the Lipan were ready, at the U.S. Army's charge Chief Castillo's group, already mounted, began to encircle the Unit and raising War Whoop-Yells began to fire their arrows and rifles at the Unit. During the battle the Lieutenant was struck twice with arrows, one on his left chest and one on his saber wielding arm, rendering him useless for combat, since he only had a saber to fight with. The arrow in the Lieutenant's left chest managed to find his pocketbook that contained some gold coins and protected him from harm.[99] Also, during the battle which lasted about 30 minutes, Corporal Wright added that Lieutenant Cosby almost met with the same fate as General George Armstrong Custer when an arrow headed towards him was intercepted by Sergeant Byrne when he tried to protect the Lieutenant and ended up with the arrow in his forehead taking him out.[100] William Wright then took command, and they ordered a retreat. Lipan Chief Castillo's group had won the battle, and he ordered his men back into the chaparral taking three of the U.S. Army's horses with them. After the battle it was noted that two more soldiers were missing (later found dead), and most of the other soldiers were wounded, some severely. Chief Castillo's group suffered three losses, which Castillo directed that they be taken away with them.[101] The U.S. soldiers later returned to Lake Trinidad where they stayed waiting for reinforcements.

Hence, the Mounted Rifle Unit which was sent to hunt down a Lipan group, the chosen ended up being Chief Castillo's group, was ill-prepared to handle such a task and were defeated at the first Battle of Lake Trinidad.

Chapter 9

Apache Victories

The Apache had several historical victories in battle. In the Battle of Cieneguilla (1854) the Jicarilla Apache along with some Ute near present day Pilar, New Mexico, ambushed and defeated a U.S. Army Cavalry Regiment known as the Dragoons in a battle that took approximately 2 hours according to witness in battle.[102] Another victory by an Apache Tribe was the Battle of Fort Buchanan (1865), an Apache attack, and victory, which led to the only captured U.S. Military post, conducted by the Chiricahua Apache in present day Santa Cruz County, Arizona.[103] During Victorio's War (1879-1880) he and his mixed Tribal group of Apaches conducted numerous successful raids and ambushes of both the Mexican and U.S. Armies.[104] The most notable battle was the Battle of Hembrillo Basin (1880), the U.S. Army advanced forces to attack the Apaches, however Victorio's group was able to evacuate the women and children and defend their position. After a long 3 days battle the U.S. Army retreated.[105] Victorio and his followers of guerrilla warfare were eventually stricken down, after many victories, at the Battle of Tres Castillos.[106]

The Lipan Apaches in particular had various encounters with other tribal Nations especially against the Comanche with outcomes in both defeat and victories. Some recorded defeats the Lipan suffered in battle were at the Battle of the Twin Villages (1759), fighting alongside the Spanish in opposition to the Comanches and Wichita's after they had burned and destroyed the Lipan Mission at San Saba[107], the Battle of Diablo Mountains (1854), where U.S. Mounted

39

Rifle force attacked Lipans at the base of the Diablo Mountains in Texas.[108] There was also General Trevino's Campaign (1878-1879) were Mexican forces launched campaigns against Lipan in Coahuila,[109] as well as the U.S. Colonel Mackenzie's Campaign to exterminate the Lipan Apache with his infamously raid at El Remolino, CU, Mexico.[110]

The Lipan did have victorious battles which were documented, most notable were the Battle of Medina (1813) with, Mexican allies, defeating the Spanish Royalist, and the Battle of Salado Creek (1839) again helping Mexican allies in defeating the Spanish Royalist. In these previous battles Lipans were just a component of the total forces against the Spanish Royalist fighting alongside mostly indigenous Mexicans and Tejanos.

The Lipan Apache had historically engaged in many battles with Native and Government allies, however this Chief Castillo Battle at Trinidad Lake has been one of the only, if not the only, documented Lipan victories over a Governmental force, the U.S. Army, where the Lipan Apache acted alone.

Chapter 10

<u>U.S. Needed Reinforcements</u>

After the routing that the U.S. Army got at the hands of Lipan Chief Castillo's group the U.S. Army sent for reinforcements, having buried their dead first. John Wright was sent to Fort Merrill to procure reinforcements and medical aid for the U.S. Army unit which took him 7 hours at a hurried pace, even killing his horse in the process.[111] John Wright was dispatched from Fort Merrill along with others to Lake Trinidad which included Dr. E.W. Johns.[112,113] On the way to lake Trinidad this dispatched Army group passed through Chief Castillo's main Lipan Apache encampment at Agua Dulce where they were settled. They rode right on through taking light gun fire from the camp but unharmed, most likely because there was only women, children, and elders there, along with a handful of warriors, and continued on to Lake Trinidad arriving the next day (May 10th) at daybreak.[114] About six warriors mounted up quickly and gave pursuit.[115] It is important to make clear that Lake Trinidad is due south-west of Fort Merrill as a crow flies. Agua Dulce is south-east of the Fort, so the U.S. Army group had to go out of their way to get to Lake Trinidad via Agua Dulce. It leads one to believe that, again, the U.S. Army knew where the main Lipan encampment was, and quite possibly passing through there to see if the Lipan warriors had gone back to camp. Let us also mention that John Wright had returned to Fort Merrill for reinforcements, but there was no word of him going through or near the Lipan encampment.

It is obvious that the Lipan warriors were not only giving pursuit to the U.S. Army detachment that rode through their encampment, but were also on the way to warn, Chief Castillo and the warriors, that more soldiers were on their way. With advanced notice Chief Castillo readied his warriors for battle. The warriors commenced putting on war paint of yellow and red. They checked and prepared their shields, some oval some round, made of thick buffalo hide doubled or triple up.[116] They needed their rifles prepped and their bow and arrows readied, they also needed to have their horses and spears ready at moment's notice.

So, while the U.S. Army was sending for reinforcements, due to the defeat that was handed to them, the Lipan Apache knew that they would return, since U.S. Army had suffered losses and their blood spilled. Castillo's group now readied themselves for what else was to come at Arroyo Baluarte (Creek).

Chapter 11

<u>Battle at Arroyo Baluarte</u>

Two days later (May 12th) Corporal William Wright and about twenty mounted rifle soldiers were dispatched to Arroyo Baluarte (Creek) from the Trinidad Lake position.[117] This time with their rifles and ammunition. The Unit came upon Lipan Chief Castillo's group at a location on Arroyo Baluarte near the Laguna Salado which was about 30 miles south of Lake Trinidad and approximately 4 miles south-east of present-day Falfurrias, Texas.[118]

[map 7 Direction of U.S. Army Travel – pg.45] With the defeat at Lake Trinidad fresh on their minds and wanting retribution, the U.S. Army immediately went on the attack. Chief Castillo's warriors were ready for what may come, now numbering about 25-30 warriors. The battle ensued with the Lipan fighting with some rifles, but mostly bows and arrows, and tomahawks. The ordeal lasted only approximately 30 minutes. At its conclusion the U.S. Army detachment had an undisclosed number killed and six wounded, some severely. The Lipan suffered four losses whom they carried away into the chaparral in retreat and some wounded who fled. This time the U.S. Army with rifles had shown to be too much of a challenge for Castillo's group.[119] The U.S. Army Mounted Rifle Unit and extra detachment from Fort Merrill however was left pretty ragged as a whole and they retreated as well, to Fort Merrill, after the encounter.[120] It would seem that this battle would have settled as a draw, since both groups had not succumbed to each other in totality, and rather, both essentially retreating.

Afterwards the reports showed that Castillo's warriors had put up a good fight, in large part to their expert equestrian and fighting skills. John Williams, (a mounted solider and eyewitness), reported, in somewhat praise, that "the Indians as a whole appearance as resembling some feat of an equestrian entertainment; the Indians performing the extraordinary evolutions as they sent their tomahawks bright glancing through the air and sent their arrows with winged speed, with a movement wonderfully rapid and graceful, resembling that of some expert violinist performing a quick and difficult piece of music." [121,122]

The second U.S. Army attack on Chief Castillo's group, this time at Arroyo Baluarte, essentially ended with both groups retreating and suffering casualties. It is safe to say that the battle ended in a draw since neither group had a decisive victory.

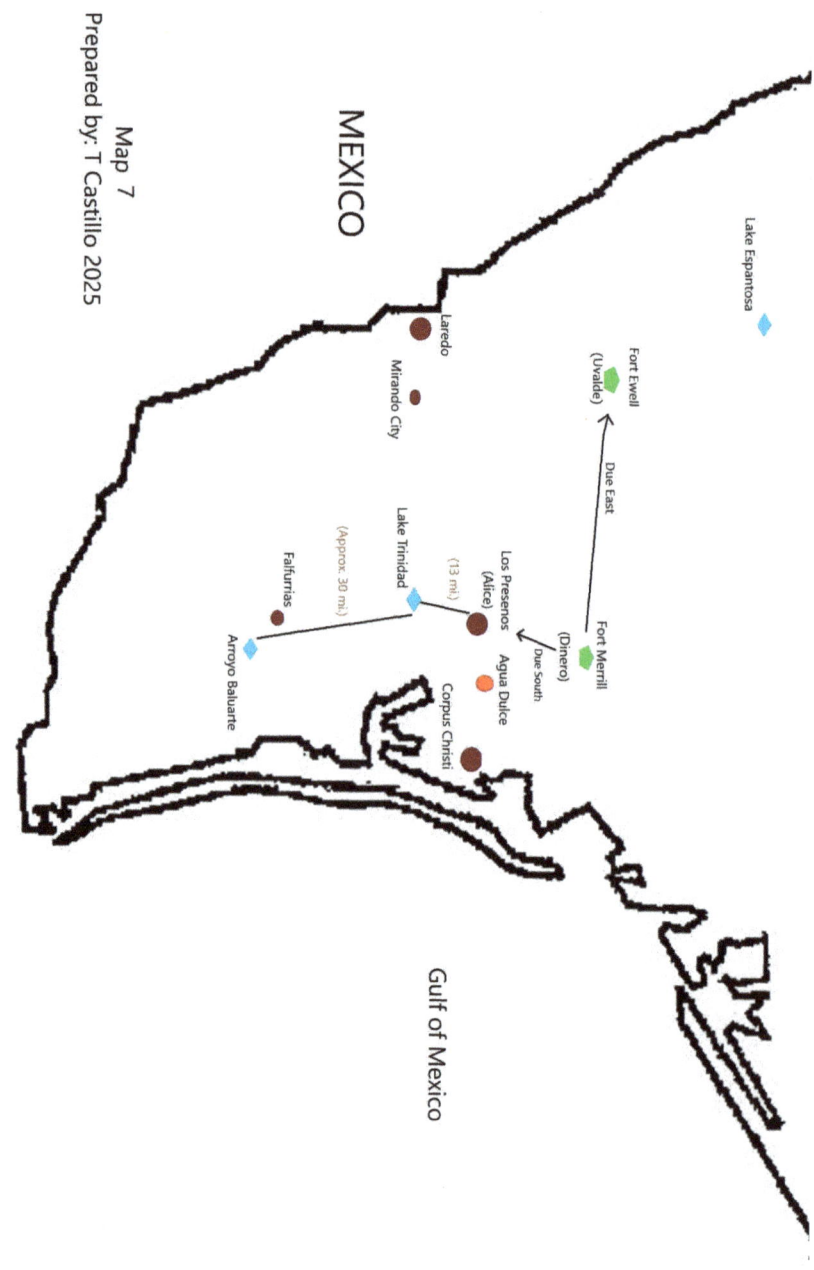

Map 7
Prepared by: T Castillo 2025

MEXICO

Lake Espantosa

Laredo

Mirando City

Fort Ewell
(Uvalde)

Due East

Falfurrias

(Approx. 30 mi.)

Lake Trinidad

(13 mi.)

Los Presenos
(Alice)

Fort Merrill
(Dinero)

Due South

Agua Dulce

Arroyo Baluarte

Corpus Christi

Gulf of Mexico

Chapter 12

U.S. Army and General Smith's Revenge

General Smith's antagonistic mentality towards the Lipan quite obviously showed itself especially after the battle at Trinidad Lake, where now U.S. Army blood had been spilled. Dated May 10th in a Message from the President to the Two Houses of Congress of the Second Session of the Thirty Third Congress General Smith Commander of the Texas Department of Defense at Corpus Christi, Texas reported, "I have already dispatched the order, a copy of which is enclosed, and **will leave no steps untaken to destroy the aggressors**." In this same letter it is stated, "Lieutenant Cosby says the guides pronounced the Indians he attacked to be Lipan and **their Chief they recognize as a man of consequence, named Castillo**."

It was now pretty evident that Chief Castillo definitely was a target. So, as relentless, and dug in as deep as he was, even if this was all initiated with false allegations, General Smith was not about to let loose of Chief Castillo, especially now that there were fallen soldiers under his command. Again, he had an "excuse", essentially brought about by his wrongful pursuit of wrongfully blamed Lipan. To further add to the malice of the U.S. Army is the fact that Indian Agent Robert S. Neighbors in February 1854 had convinced congress to pass legislation to establish reservations for the Indians of Texas. But instead of attempting to move Castillo's group to the new Texas Reservations, they proceeded to go after and attack Castillo's group.[123]

[Picture 4] *"Lipan Warrior"*
Source: Open Domain
Credit: According to Dessin de Gilbert, Photo by J. Laurent
(1842 – Mexico)

Chapter 13
<u>Lipan Beliefs Used Against Them</u>

Circling back to the Lipan spiritualism which ties into their Peyote culture at the time, it could have very well been used against them. The nuances and details of the Lipan spiritualism, to my knowledge have never been reviled and it is not my place to do so here. What is important here is knowing that from the beginning of this ordeal the Lipan people would have been turning to ceremonies to deal with these life events as they always had. To the Lipan there is a time to pray for peace, for hunting, for health, for wellness, for political/diplomatic endeavors, for special life events, and for war. Since these spiritual ceremonies are tied into celestial occurrences some are cyclical, while others were done as events unfolded. [124] In the case of peace/diplomacy and war both practices are instituted. There is a time of peace/diplomacy and a time of war, yet war could come at any time. Both depend on various factors, and as they say, "timing is everything".

It is important here to interject that the U.S. Army employed Native Americans in the capacity of scouts and trackers. This was the case when the U.S. Army went after Chief Castillo and his group. And we know that the Native American scouts/trackers which were deployed to find Lipan Chief Castillo were LIPAN and that they were promised to receive gifts of great value if they helped find Castillo's group.[125] Realistically one could understand the position these Lipan scouts would have been in. At a time when many of the Lipan groups/bands, now a broken people, and on the verge of starvation, it would not have taken much for the U.S. Government and U.S. Army to convince Lipan men to be scouts in exchange for these "valuable gifts" which could help their families.[126] To Lipans it could have been a difficult decision, to either help their own starving peoples or help the U.S. Army and betray other Lipan peoples. As this history unraveled, the latter prevailed.

 Be it as it may these Lipan scouts would have known the spiritual ways of their people. It would seem that the U.S. Army could have known, quite possibly through the aid of the Lipan scout's knowledge, when it would be best time to go after Lipan Chief Castillo and his group, especially if given an "excuse". It would have been to the U.S. Army's advantage to attack at a time, that according to the Lipan beliefs was for peace and therefor, they would be in an amicable state. Without going into any undisclosed detail, we Lipan know that in 1854 that time began on July 10 and that ceremony would have been on or near that date, and that a pilgrimage to the Peyote Gardens in the Laredo vicinity would have taken place to collect the Peyote Medicine for that ceremony.

 [picture 5 Peyote - The Medicine – pg.51]

It is easy to conclude that the U.S. Army used the timing of ritual ceremonies as a military strategy against the Lipan.

Chapter 14
Peyote Harvest Pilgrimages

Next, we need to address the importance of Peyote to the Lipan Apache. It is well documented that the Lipan practiced Peyotism in ceremony.[127,128,129,130,131] As stated before Lipan would hold ceremony for various reasons, war, peace, hunt, political situations, celestial events, and special events.[132] For these events the Lipan would need to travel to the Peyote Gardens, usually several in a group, to pray, and harvest the "medicine", Peyote. The Lipan were not the only ones to make pilgrimages to the Laredo area to collect Peyote.[133] Many other Native American affiliated groups also make these pilgrimages to the Peyote gardens, even still today.[134]

So, let us now consider how Lipan Chief Castillo's group would have traveled to go on these Pilgrimages. We know that the area that Chief Castillo's group frequented was from what is today the Agua Dulce, Alice, and Kingsville area in South Texas. I would also say that the Ceremonial Grounds for Chief Castillo's group were in the Lake Trinidad and/or Arroyo Baluarte vicinities. With that in mind the group would have had to travel just about due **West** to get to the Peyote gardens, then return due **East**.

map 4 Traveled Directions pg.24;
map 8 Texas Peyote Gardens pg.52]

The pilgrimages for the ceremonies involved would have given the U.S. Army another false excuse, via tracking, to pursue them, picking up the Lipan "tracks" as they returned from the peyote gardens headed east.

[Picture 5] "*Peyote – The Medicine*"
Courtesy: Andres Gutierrez Camarillo

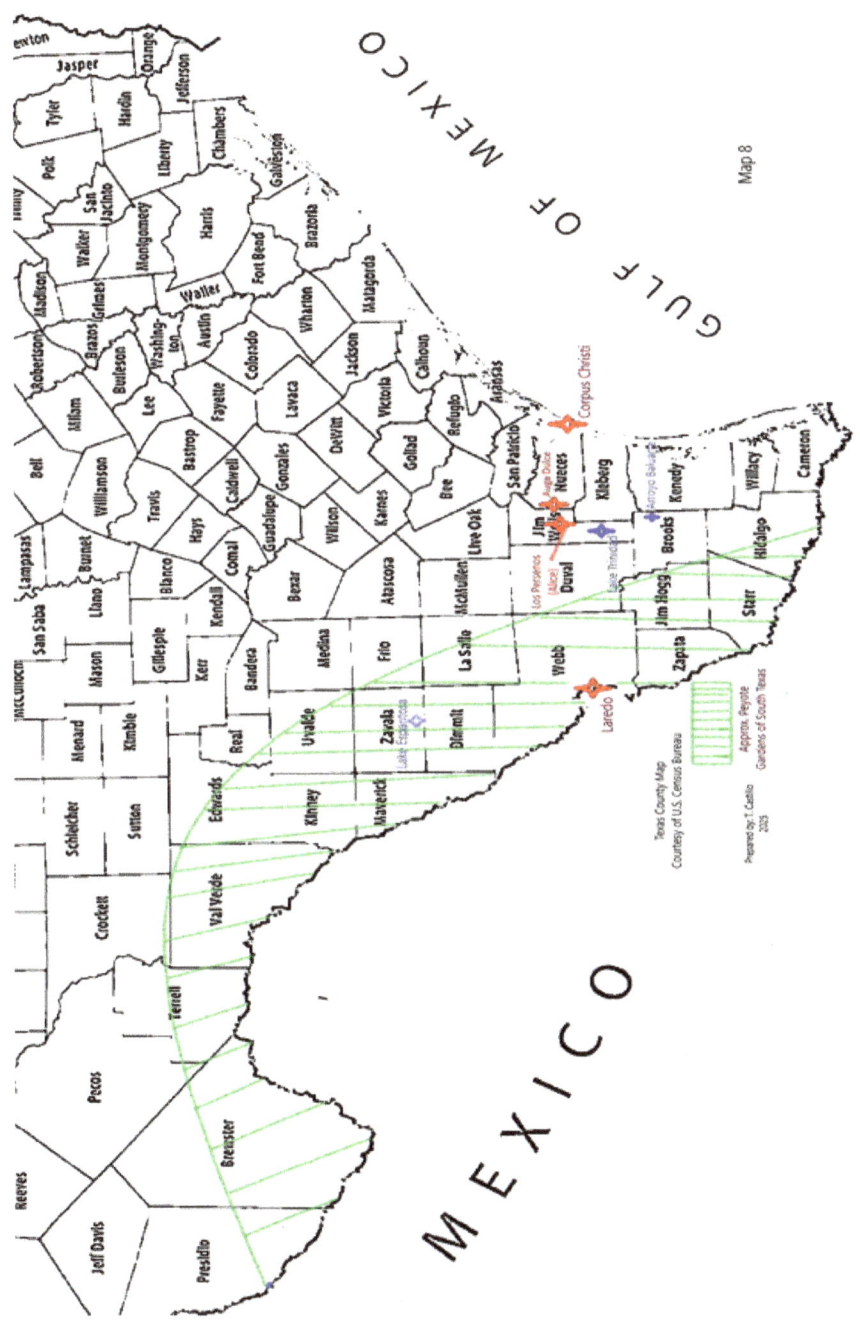

Map 8

Texas County Map
Courtesy of U.S. Census Bureau

Prepared by: T. Castillo
2005

Approx. Peyote
Gardens of South Texas

Chapter 15

The Last Battle for Lipan Chief Castillo

(2nd Battle at Lake Trinidad)

According to General's P.F. Smith's Report from the Headquarters at Corpus Christi, Texas for the Department of Defense dated July 15, 1854, which was included in the President of the United States' Message to the Second Session of the Thirty Third Congress, he stated that a mounted rifle unit was sent towards the "Rio Grande" on July 4th, 1854, it was headed **South** to the boarder from Fort Inge. Heading **south** from Fort Inge would take the unit directly towards Laredo, Texas. Lead by Captain (Michael) Van Buren the Mounted Rifle Unit picked up a trail after encountering an 8th Infantry unit near Lake Espantosa out of Fort Clarke who were following a trail from the "northward". Captain Van Buren's unit then proceeded to take up the trail "**southward**".

Here is the discrepancy. The only possible way that they could have ended up at Lipan Chief Castillo's group is if they headed **East** at some point and then for quite a distance. According to the letter General Smith states that Captain Van Buren's unit found Chief Castillo's group about 13 miles Southwest of "Proscenius" (Los Preseños, Texas) now Alice, Texas which is exactly where Lake Trinidad is located.[135] Lake Trinidad is located almost exactly due **East** of Laredo, Texas. This would have put them on a path that, as stated earlier, would have been the path Chief Castillo's pilgrimage from the Peyote gardens would have taken them back to Lake Trinidad. [map 4 Traveled Directions Pg.24] So, this adds doubt as to exactly where Captain Van Buren's unit was heading, or for what reason. Let us also keep in mind the disdain that General Smith had with Lipan Chief Castillo's group since the U.S. Army had suffered a loss, and what is effectively a draw in battles, as well as needing justifications demanded by the citizens of Laredo.

Again, Captain Van Buren's Mounted Rifle unit left Fort Inge on July 4th, 1854, however they attacked Lipan Chief Castillo's group at Lake Trinidad on July 11th, 1854, one week later. According to Google Maps it is estimated to take just under 3 days on foot! Therefor Captain Van Buren's Mounted Rifle unit would have reached Lipan Chief Castillo's group at Lake Trinidad by the 7th of July, If on foot. So why wait till July 11th, 1854, to attack?

A very viable reason the U.S. Army's Mounted Rifle unit waited nearby would be due to military tactics. It is known that the unit had among its troops a Lipan Apache Scout.[136] This scout would have had privy to the Lipan ceremonial and celestial events that could be used to find Chief Castillo's group in a solemn state under a full moon. As stated before, July 10th held a special meaning for the Lipan, it was the beginning of a particular time for peace.[137] Hence July 11th would have been good military strategy to attack Lipan Chief Castillo's group.

July 11th was indeed the day that Captain Van Buren chooses to attack Lipan Chief Castillo and his group at Lake Trinidad, Texas. The U.S. Army decision to attack Chief Castillo's group, again, at Lake Trinidad, could have also added to a military tactic due to the ceremonial sacredness Lake Trinidad held, and therefore an added sociological advantage. The length of the battle is unknown. However, what we can gather is that during the battle Lipan Chief

Castillo was Killed, and his body was taken away by the U.S. Army to an undisclosed location and which is quite possibly classified. Chief Castillo's group fought to regain the body, but they were not able to get it back.[138] The Mounted Rifle Unit lost an unknown number of troops and had several wounded as well, so much so that the unit could not pursue the retreating Lipan group. During the battle Captain Van Buren was shot in the abdomen with an arrow and unable to be moved, succumbed to his wound a few days later. [139,140] In less than a year, after Lipan Chief Castillo was killed, and the remnants' of the Sun Otter Band disbursed, Major General Persifor Frazier Smith had the Texas Army Headquarters moved back to San Antonio from Corpus Christi. Corpus Christi served as the Texas Army Headquarters from Fall 1852 until Spring 1855.

It is significant to note that the Indian depredations did not recede after the killing of Lipan Chief Castillo and the disbursement of the remnants of the Sun Otter Band of South Texas. The depredations continued with the State of Texas and U.S. Governments acknowledging that they were being conducted by those known to had carried them out all along.[141,142,143,144]

Summary

The mentality of the U.S. Army can be summed up with a passage in Gary Clayton Anderson's (1948) "The Conquest of TEXAS": ethnic cleansing in the promised land, 1820-1875" (pg. 254), in 1853, "Indian agent Howard, knowing Manuel's Lipan band, could hardly believe the news."(of an attack) "He knew, as did the army, that groups consisting of renegade Mexican and Americans frequently crossed the Rio Grande to steal. Howard noted often in his correspondence that they "dressed in the Indian garb" and were responsible for most of the "reported Indian outrages." The Lipan Manuel and his people, numbering perhaps two hundred, Howard soon discovered, at the time of the attack, were actually visiting Fort Mason, some two hundred miles to the northwest. This news failed to reach Colonel Harney, who still sought Indian blood. The Colonel immediately ordered his troops to "attack the tribe" and "to **exterminate**, if possible, every man in it, and make prisoners of the women and children.""

It would seem that General Persifor F. Smith was feeling pressure to get some kind of justice for the citizens of Laredo for the depredations and killings, which also included the surrounding areas, so he needed to persecute the accused, even though falsely accused, the Lipan Apaches. He knew that the perpetrators came from the north, so he initially went after the Lipan de Arriba at Fort Inge. When that didn't pan out because government officials testified that the Lipan de Arriba had alibis, he went after Lipans that were in the vicinity of the Headquarters of Department of Defense in Corpus Christi, where he was in command, the Lipan de Abajo. He, knowing that Chief Castillo and his group were in the area, decided to go after them. Again, it is quite possible that it was done to satisfy the citizens of the Laredo area. Adding to that, another reason could have been to make sure that Chief Castillo's group would not cause any problems or uprisings in the future so near to the Headquarters.[145] He found out that Chief Castillo's group was a force to contend with, but as it seems he was too proud to back away and needed to do as the U.S. government wanted, to clear the lands of Indians whomever they may be. However, in the process he handed Lipan Chief Castillo one of the only documented Lipan vs. U.S. Army victory.

Final Word

This project's purpose is to establish that Chief Castillo did not die in vain and will be noted in history. He fought alongside his warriors to protect his group and their way of life. The end result was the surviving remnants of the Sun Otter group were scattered like smoke into the wind. Chief Castillo in his previous directions, if he would not return, had also left instructions to send his son far away, to New Mexico, if need be. Some of the group stayed in the surrounding area and assimilated, some went to Mexico and some disbursed to different parts of Texas and the U.S. His own son was sent to live in New Mexico with relatives.

Thanks to his guidance, of the historically last documented free Sun Otter group, since Chief Magoosh had already disbursed the Sun Otter Band in 1950 and took his group to the Mescalero reservation,[146,147] and even though he perished, "The Lipan… Are still here, in survival mode..."

Tom BearClaw Castillo, father to the 7th generation of Lipan Chief Castillo

Notes and Citations:

1) Tucker, Spencer C. (2011) "The Encyclopedia of North American Indian Wars 1607-1890"Pg. 442

2) Myer to James, February 14, 1855 in Clary, "Myer Letters", 42

3) Note: Referenced here as a "clan" since the Sun Otter Band which had been lead by Chief Magoosh was disbanded by him prior in 1850. This seems to be the last documented remnants of the Sun Otter band in their original homelands.

4) Perez, Gary (2024) – Interview Conducted by T. Castillo "Peyote and the Indigenous of South Texas and Northern Mexico"

5) Habig, Marion A. (1968) "The Alamo Chain of Missions: A History of San Antonio's Five Old Missions" pgs. 52-67

6) Robinson, Sherry (2013) "I Fought a Good Fight: A History of the Lipan Apaches" pgs. 345-353

7) Ray, Verne F. & Opler, Morris E. (1974) "Apache Indians X: Ethnohistorical Analysis of Documents Relating to the Apache Indians of Texas/ Lipan and Mescalero Apache in Texas" pg. 307

8) McGown-Minor, Nancy (2009) "Turning Adversity to Advantage: A History of The Lipan Apaches of Texas and Northern Mexico, 1700-1900" pg. 164-165

9) McGown-Minor, Nancy (2009) "Turning Adversity to Advantage: A History of The Lipan Apaches of Texas and Northern Mexico, 1700-1900" pg. 165

10) Newcomb Jr., W.W. (1961) "The Indians of Texas: From Prehistoric to Modern Times" pg. 116

11) Edge, Laura B (2016) "The Lipan Apache" pg. 18

12) Robinson, Sherry (2013) "I Fought a Good Fight: A History of the Lipan Apaches" pg. 230

13) Robinson, Sherry (2013) "I Fought a Good Fight: A History of the Lipan Apaches" pg. 233

14) Schilz, Thomas F. (1987) "Lipan Apaches of Texas" pgs. 3-4

15) Brown Jr., Tom (1993) "Grandfather: A Native American's lifelong search for truth and harmony with nature" pgs. 2-3

16) Edge, Laura B (2016) "The Lipan Apache" pg. 14

17) National Park Service Article: [https://www.nps.gov/articles/000/what-happened-to-the-bison.htm]

18) Dan Flores "Bison Ecology and Bison Diplomacy; The Southern Plains from 1800 to 1850", *The Journal of American History* 78 no.2 (September 1991) 465-85

19) Phillis Morgan "Buffalo on the Santa Fe Trail" *Wagon Tracks* 18, no. 3 (May 2004): 7-8

20) Anderson, Gary C. (2005) "The Conquest of Texas: Ethnic

Cleansing in the Promised Land, 1820-1875 pg. 258

21) Google AI Overview 3/3/2025 "Were Lipan Teepees made of Canvas?"

22) Newcomb Jr., W.W. (1961) "The Indians of Texas: From Prehistoric to Modern Times" pg. 109-110

23) Google AI Overview 3/3/2025 "Did Lipan use blankets?"

24) Britten, Thomas (2009) "Lipan Apaches: People of Wind and Lighting" pg. 63

25) Smallwood, James M. (2004) "The Indian Texans" pg. 58

26) McGown-Minor, Nancy (2009) "The Light Gray People: An Ethno-History of the Lipan Apaches of Texas and Northern Mexico" pg.87

27) Moorhead, Max L. (1968) "The Apache Frontier: Jacobo Ugarte and Spanish-Indian Relations in Northern New Spain, 1769-1791" pgs. 259-269

28) Wooster, Robert (1995) "Recollections of Western Texas: 1852-55" pg. 86

29) Weber, David J. (1982) "THE MEXICAN FRONTIER 1821-1846: The American Southwest Under Mexico" pg. 87

30) Loughery, Robert W. The Texas Republican (Marshall, TX), Vol. 5, No. 46, Ed. 1 Saturday, June 10, 1854, newspaper, June 10, 1854; [https://texashistory.unt.edu/ark:/67531etapth1094930/m1/2/:] (accessed January 21, 2025), University of North Texas Libraries, The Portal to Texas History, texashistory.unit.edu; .

31) Google AI Overview 3/7/2025 "What would be the breakdown of a Native American group of 100?"

32) Note: Taken into consideration a proportion to 100 and the mortality rate at the time of Native Americans (Google AI Overview 3/7/2025 "Mortality rate for Native Americans in 1850's")

33) McGown-Minor, Nancy (2009) "The Light Gray People: An Ethno-History of the Lipan Apaches of Texas and Northern Mexico" pg. 80

34) Note: Since Lipan Chief Castillo is known to have at least 1 child (Jose Pablo Castillo) it leads to the fact that he indeed had at least one wife.

35) Emilio Castillo (June 10, 2006) Interview conducted by T. Castillo "The Castillo family oral history by Emilio Castillo."

36) Johnson, Michael G. (2013) "American Indian Tribes of the Southwest" pg. 13

37) Britten, Thomas A. (2009) "The Lipan Apaches: People of Wind and Lighting" pg. 215

38) Loughery, Robert W. The Texas Republican (Marshall, TX), Vol. 5, No. 37, Ed. 1 Saturday, April 8,1854, newspaper, April 8, 1854; [https://texashistory.unt.edu/ark:/67531/metapth1095293/m1/2/:](accessed January 21, 2025), University of North Texas Libraries, The Portal to Texas History, texashistory.unit.edu; .

39) Winfrey, Dorman H. & Day, James (1995) "Texas Indian Papers"

Vol. V pg. 160

40) Loughery, Robert W. The Texas Republican (Marshall, TX),
Vol. 5, No. 37, Ed. 1 Saturday, April 8,1854, newspaper, April 8,
1854; [https://texashistory.unt.edu/ark:/67531/metapth1095293/
m1/2/:](accessed January 21, 2025), University of North Texas
Libraries, The Portal to Texas History, texashistory.unit.edu; .

41) Winfrey, Dorman H. & Day, James (1995) "Texas Indian
Papers" Vol. V pg. 160

42) Loughery, Robert W. The Texas Republican (Marshall, TX),
Vol. 5, No. 37, Ed. 1 Saturday, April 8,1854, newspaper, April
8, 1854; [https://texashistory.unt.edu/ark:/67531/
etapth1095293/m1/2/:](accessed January 21, 2025),
University of North Texas Libraries, The Portal to Texas
History, texashistory.unit.edu; .

43) Winfrey, Dorman H. & Day, James (1995) "Texas Indian Papers"
Vol. V pg. 160, 166

44) Winfrey, Dorman H. & Day, James (1995) "Texas Indian Papers"
Vol. V pg. 161

45) Loughery, Robert W. The Texas Republican (Marshall, TX), Vol
5, No. 37, Ed. 1 Saturday, April 8,1854, newspaper, April 8,1854;
[https://texashistory.unt.edu/ark:/67531/metapth1095293/m1/2/:]
(accessed January 21, 2025), University of North Texas Libraries, The
Portal to Texas History, texashistory.unit.edu; .

46) Winfrey, Dorman H. & Day, James (1995) "Texas Indian Papers"
Vol. V pg. 161

47) Winfrey, Dorman H. & Day, James (1995) "Texas Indian Papers"
Vol. V pg. 161

48) Newcomb Jr., W. W. (1961) "The Indians of Texas: From
Prehistoric to Modern Times" pg. 130

49) Britten, Thomas (2009) "The Lipan Apaches: People of Wind
and Lighting" pg. 144

50) McGown-Minor, Nancy (2009) "The Light Gray People: An
Ethno-History of the Lipan Apaches of
Texas and Northern Mexico" pg. 165-166

51) McGown-Minor, Nancy (2009) "The Light Gray People: An Ethno-
History of the Lipan Apaches of Texas and Northern Mexico"
pg. 164-165

52) Grimm (1976,2020) "Los Presenos, TX"; Texas State Historical
Association [http://www.tshaonline.org/handbook/entries/los-
presenos-tx]

53) Moore (2021) "Los Presenos"; The Historical Marker Database;
[https://www.hmdb.org/m.asp?m=180612]

54) Grimm (1952,1994) "Collins, TX (Nueces County)"; Texas State
Historical Association[https://www.tshaonline.org/handbook/entries/
collins-tx-nueces-county]

55) Major General P.F. Smith (July 15, 1854) Report from Headquarters
Dept. of Defense, TX, included in "Message from President of U.S. to
Congress at the Commencement of the Second Session of the Thirty-
Third Congress."

56) Britten, Thomas (2009) "The Lipan Apaches: People of Wind and Lighting" pg. 144

57) Winfrey, Dorman H. & Day, James (1995) "Texas Indian Papers" Vol. V pg.160-161

58) Loughery, Robert W. The Texas Republican (Marshall, Tx), Vol. 5, No. 37, Ed. 1 Saturday, April 8, 1854, newspaper, April 8, 1854; [https://texashistory.unt.edu/ark:/67531/metapth1095293/m1/2/:] (accessed January 21, 2025), University of North Texas Libraries, The Portal to Texas History, texashistory.unit.edu; .

59) Winfrey, Dorman H. & Day, James (1995) "Texas Indian Papers" Vol. V pg. 161

60) Robinson, Sherri (2013) "I Fought a Good Fight: A History of the Lipan Apaches" pg. 242

61) Winfrey, Dorman H. & Day, James (1995) "Texas Indian Papers" Vol. V pg. 165

62) Winfrey, Dorman H. & Day, James (1995) "Texas Indian Papers" Vol. V pg. 159-160

63) Winfrey, Dorman H. & Day, James (1995) "Texas Indian Papers" Vol. V pg. 160

64) Winfrey, Dorman H. & Day, James (1995) "Texas Indian Papers" Vol. V pg. 161

65) Winfrey, Dorman H. & Day, James (1995) "Texas Indian Papers" Vol. V pg. 161

66) Robinson, Sherry (2013) "I Fought a Good Fight: A History of the Lipan Apaches" pg. 242

67) Winfrey, Dorman H. & Day, James (1995) "Texas Indian Papers" Vol. V pg. 162

68) Winfrey, Dorman H. & Day, James (1995) "Texas Indian Papers" Vol. V pg. 159

69) Loughery, Robert W. The Texas Republican (Marshall, Tx), Vol. 5, No. 37, Ed. 1 Saturday, April 8, 1854, newspaper, April 8, 1854; [https://texashistory.unt.edu/ark:/67531/metapth1095293/m1/2/:] (accessed January 21, 2025), University of North Texas Libraries, The Portal to Texas History, texashistory.unit.edu; .

70) Winfrey, Dorman H. & Day, James (1995) "Texas Indian Papers" Vol. V pg. 164-165

71) Loughery, Robert W. The Texas Republican (Marshall, Tx), Vol. 5, No. 37, Ed. 1 Saturday, April 8, 1854, newspaper, April 8, 1854; [https://texashistory.unt.edu/ark:/67531/metapth1095293/m1/2/:] (accessed January 21, 2025), University of North Texas Libraries, The Portal to Texas History, texashistory.unit.edu; .

72) Loughery, Robert W. The Texas Republican (Marshall, Tx), Vol. 5, No. 37, Ed. 1 Saturday, April 8, 1854, newspaper, April 8, 1854; [https://texashistory.unt.edu/ark:/67531/metapth1095293/m1/2/:] (accessed January 21, 2025), University of North Texas Libraries, The Portal to Texas History, texashistory.unit.edu; .

73) Robinson, Sherry (2013) "I Fought a Good Fight: A History of the Lipan Apaches" pg. 242

74) Winfrey, Dorman H. & Day, James (1995) "Texas Indian Papers"

Vol. V pg. 165

75) Ray, Verne F. & Opler, Morris E. (1974) "Apache Indians X: Ethnohistorical Analysis of Documents Relating to the Apache Indians of Texas/ Lipan and Mescalero Apache in Texas" pg. 145-146

76) Ray, Verne F. & Opler, Morris E. (1974) "Apache Indians X: Ethnohistorical Analysis of Documents Relating to the Apache Indians of Texas/ Lipan and Mescalero Apache in Texas"" pg. 145

77) Ray, Verne F. & Opler, Morris E. (1974) "Apache Indians X: Ethnohistorical Analysis of Documents Relating to the Apache Indians of Texas/ Lipan and Mescalero Apache in Texas"" pg. 146

78) Ray, Verne F. & Opler, Morris E. (1974) "Apache Indians X: Ethnohistorical Analysis of Documents Relating to the Apache Indians of Texas/ Lipan and Mescalero Apache in Texas"" pg. 145

79) Anderson, Gary C. (2005) "The Conquest of Texas: Ethnic Cleansing in the Promised Land, 1820-1875 pg. 269

80) Winfrey, Dorman H. & Day, James (1995) "Texas Indian Papers" Vol. V pg. 164-166

81) Loughery, Robert W. The Texas Republican (Marshall, Tx), Vol. 5, No. 37, Ed. 1 Saturday, April 8, 1854, newspaper, April 8, 1854; [https://texashistory.unt.edu/ark:/67531/metapth1095293/m1/2/:] (accessed January 21, 2025), University of North Texas Libraries, The Portal to Texas History, texashistory.unit.edu; .

82) Anderson, Gary C. (2005) "The Conquest of Texas: Ethnic Cleansing in the Promised Land, 1820-1875 pg. 264

83) Britten, Thomas (2009) "The Lipan Apache: People of Wind and Lighting" pg. 215

84) McGown-Minor, Nancy (2009) "Turning Adversity to Advantage: A History of The Lipan Apaches of Texas and Northern Mexico, 1700-1900" pg. 165

85) McGown-Minor, Nancy (2009) "The Light Gray People: An Ethno-History of the Lipan Apaches of Teas and Northern Mexico" pgs.106-108

86) Bigelow, Michael E., Command Historian (July-September 2012) "A Short History of Army Intelligence" U.S. Army Intelligence and Security Command.[irp.fas.org/agency/army/short.pdf]

87) Britten, Thomas (2009) "The Lipan Apaches: People of Wind and Lighting" pg. 215

88) Major General P.F. Smith (May 10, 1854) Report from Headquarters Dept. of Defense, TX, included in "Message from President of U.S. to Congress at the Commencement of the Second Session of the Thirty-Third Congress."

89) Ray, Verne F. & Opler, Morris E. (1974) "Apache Indians X: Ethnohistorical Analysis of Documents Relating to the Apache Indians of Texas/ Lipan and Mescalero Apache in Texas"" pg. 145

90) Givens, Murphy, "The Day that Company B left for the Korean War", Corpus Christi Caller-Times, October 11, 2016

91) Robinson, Sherry (2013) "I Fought a Good Fight: A History of the Lipan Apaches" pg. 242

92) Major General P.F. Smith (May 10, 1854) Report from

Headquarters Dept. of Defense, TX, included in "Message from President of U.S. to Congress at the Commencement of the Second Session of the Thirty-Third Congress."

93) Robinson, Sherry (2013) "I Fought a Good Fight: A History of the Lipan Apaches" pg. 242

94) Major General P.F. Smith (May 10, 1854) Report from Headquarters Dept. of Defense, TX, included in "Message from President of U.S. to Congress at the Commencement of the Second Session of the Thirty-Third Congress."

95) Wooster, Robert (1995) "Recollections of Western Texas: 1852-55" pg. 83

96) Robinson, Sherri (2013) "I Fought a Good Fight: A History of the Lipan Apaches" pg. 242

97) Wooster, Robert (1995) "Recollections of Western Texas: 1852-55" pg. 82-83

98) Wooster, Robert (1995) "Recollections of Western Texas: 1852-55" pg. 83

99) Wooster, Robert (1995) "Recollections of Western Texas: 1852-55" pg. 84

100) Loughery, Robert W. The Texas Republican (Marshall, Tx), Vol. 5, No. 46, Ed. 1 Saturday, June 10, 1854, newspaper, June 10, 1854; [https://texashistory.unt.edu/ark:/67531/metapth1094930/m1/2/:] (accessed January 21, 2025), University of North Texas Libraries, The Portal to Texas History, texashistory.unit.edu; .

101) Wooster, Robert (1995) "Recollections of Western Texas: 1852-55" pg. 85

102) Gorenfeld, Will (5/15/2018) "The Battle of Cieneguilla : Dragoons vs. Jicarilla Apaches"[https://www.historynet.com/battle-cieneguilla-dragoons-vs-jicarilla-apaches/]

103) Alonzo, Alexander (7/8/2022) "Until It's Too Late: The Battle of Fort Buchanan" [https://www.arizonacivilwarcouncil.com/post/until-its-too-late]

104) Utley, Robert M. (9/3/2008) "Victorio's War"[https://www.historynet.com/victorios-war/]

105) Laumbach, Karl W. (2002) "An Apache Battlefield of the Victorio's War" pgs. 175-239

106) Laumbach, Karl W. (2002) "An Apache Battlefield of the Victorio's War" pgs. 250-251

107) Williams, Chad (1/15/2010) "Twin Villages, Battle of the ", The Encyclopedia of Oklahoma History and Culture, [https://www.okhistory.org/publications/enc/entry?entry=TW005]

108) Wikipedia. (2009) "Battle of Diablo Mountains" Last modified January 22, 2025. [https://en.m.wiipedia.org/wiki/Battle_of_the_Diablo_Mountains]

109) McGown-Minor, Nancy (2009) "Turning Adversity to Advantage: A History of The Lipan Apaches of Texas and Northern Mexico, 1700-1900" pg. 188-190

110) McGown-Minor, Nancy (2009) "Turning Adversity to Advantage: A History of The Lipan Apaches of Texas and Northern Mexico,

1700-1900" pgs. 181-184

111) Wooster, Robert (1995) "Recollections of Western Texas: 1852-55" pg. 85

112) Major General P.F. Smith (May 10, 1854) Report from Headquarters Dept. of Defense, TX, included in "Message from President of U.S. to Congress at the Commencement of the Second Session of the Thirty-Third Congress."

113) Wooster, Robert (1995) "Recollections of Western Texas: 1852-55" pg. 86

114) Travis, Michael "Arroyo Baluarte" [https://www.forttours.com/pages/ arroyobaluarte.asp]

115) Wooster, Robert (1995) "Recollections of Western Texas: 1852-55" pg. 86

116) Robinson, Sherry (2013) "I Fought a Good Fight: A History of the Lipan Apaches" pgs. 242-243

117) Michno, Gregory F. and Michno, Susan. J. (2008) "forgotten Fights: Little-Known Raids and Skirmishes on the Frontier, 1823-1890" Pg. 125

118) Wooster, Robert (1995) "Recollections of Western Texas: 1852-55" pg. 86

119) Wooster, Robert (1995) "Recollections of Western Texas: 1852-55" pg. 87

120) Travis, Michael "Arroyo Baluarte" [https://www.forttours.com/pages/ arroyobaluarte.asp]

121) Travis, Michael "Arroyo Baluarte" [https://www.forttours.com/pages/ arroyobaluarte.asp]

122) Robinson, Sherry (2013) "I Fought a Good Fight: A History of the Lipan Apaches" pg. 243

123) Smith, F. Todd (2005) "From Dominance to Disappearance: The Indians of Texas and the near Southwest, 786-1559" pg. 213

124) Parke, Aubrey G., (2020) "Stories from the River". Sociology and Anthropology Honors Theses. 13. pg. 65 [https://digitalcommos. trinity.edu/socanthro_honors/13]

125) Oldham, W. S. & Marshall, John. Texas State Gazette. (Austin, Tex.), Vol. 5, No. 52, Ed. 1, Saturday, August 19, 1854, newspaper, August 19, 1854; Austin, Texas. [https://texashistory.unt.edu/ark:/67531/ metapth81148/:] (accessed June 11, 2025), University of North Texas Libraries, The Portal to Texas History, https://texashistory.unt.edu; crediting The Dolph Briscoe Center for American History.

126) Britten, Thomas (2009) "The Lipan Apaches: People of Wind and Lighting" pg. 215

127) Britten, Thomas (2009) "The Lipan Apaches: People of Wind and Lighting" pgs. 18, 21

128) Robinson, Sherry (2013) "I Fought a Good Fight: A History of the Lipan Apaches" pgs. 4, 77

129) McGown-Minor, Nancy (2009) "The Light Gray People: An Ethno-History of the Lipan Apaches of Texas and Northern Mexico" pgs. 97, 144

130) Opler, Morris E. (1940) "Myths and Legends of the Lipan Apache

Indians" pgs. 56-58

131) Schaefer, Stacy B. (2015) "Amada's Blessings from the Peyote Gardens of South Texas"   pg. 34

132) Perez, Gary (2024) – Interview Conducted by T. Castillo "Peyote and the Indigenous of South Texas and Northern Mexico"

133) Parke, Aubrey G., (2020) "Stories from the River". Sociology and Anthropology Honors Theses. 13. pg. 65 [https://digitalcommos. trinity.edu/socanthro_honors/13]

134) Schaefer, Stacy B. (2015) "Amada's Blessings from the Peyote Gardens of South Texas" pgs. 93,94,105

135) Major General P.F. Smith (July 15, 1854) Report from Headquarters Dept. of Defense, TX, included in "Message from President of U.S. to Congress at the Commencement of the Second Session of the Thirty-Third Congress."

136) Major General P.F. Smith (May 10, 1854 & July 15, 1854) Reports from Headquarters Dept. of Defense, TX, included in "Message from President of U.S. to Congress at the Commencement of the Second Session of the Thirty-Third Congress."

137) Perez, Gary (2024) – Interview Conducted by T. Castillo "Peyote and the Indigenous of South Texas and Northern Mexico"

138) Wagner, Frank (2021) "Biography by Frank Wagner", City of Corpus Christi Public Libraries, Old Bayview Cemetery – Michael E. Van Buren [https://obc.cclibraries.com/list/tv/van-buren-michael-e]

139) Major General P.F. Smith (July 15, 1854) Reports from Headquarters Dept. of Defense, TX, included in "Message from President of U.S. to Congress at the Commencement of the Second Session of the Thirty-Third Congress."

140) Wagner, Frank (2021) "Biography by Frank Wagner", City of Corpus Christi Public Libraries, Old Bayview Cemetery – Michael E. Van Buren [https://obc.cclibraries.com/list/tv/van-buren-michael-e]

141) Winfrey, Dorman H. And Day, James M. (1995) "The Indian Papers of Texas and the Southwest 1825-1916" Vol V pgs. 185-187

142) Winfrey, Dorman H. And Day, James M. (1995) "The Indian Papers of Texas and the Southwest 1825-1916" Vol V pgs. 190-191

143) Winfrey, Dorman H. And Day, James M. (1995) "The Indian Papers of Texas and the Southwest 1825-1916" Vol V pgs. 194-195

144) Winfrey, Dorman H. And Day, James M. (1995) "The Indian Papers of Texas and the Southwest 1825-1916" Vol V pgs. 197-198

145) Schroder, Eric: U.S. Army Coronal retired, Interview by: T. Castillo (3/2/2025) "Chief Castillo's Missing Body".

146) McGown-Minor, Nancy (2009) "Turning Adversity to Advantage: A History of The Lipan Apaches of Texas and Northern Mexico, 1700-1900" pg. 162

147) McGown-Minor, Nancy (2009) "Turning Adversity to Advantage: A History of The Lipan Apaches of Texas and Northern Mexico, 1700-1900" pg. 156

Part II
My Ancestral Journey

Table of Contents
Part II

My Ancestral Journey

Table of Contents Cont'd

Lipan Chief Castillo – 1854 / My Ancestral Journey

Citations and Credits:

My Ancestral Journey

Preface

As you relive this journey with me it will be apparent that it was not an easy one. It took time, patience, perseverance, rest, and special occurrences. You undoubtedly will, or do, understand that journeys like this can leave you exhausted, disappointed, excited, sad, and hopefully fulfilled. This journey that you take with me is one I have endured yet persevered through. A journey such as this will test your ability to piecemeal information from various sources and references to gain inferences which can lead to other discoveries. It will make great use of your memory and the ability to regurgitate times, places, and situations to clarify and add merit to these inferences.

I hope it will inspire you to initiate your own or rekindle one you possibly have already been on. As you will see I encountered some, what can only be described as occurrences. The occurrences that I encountered during this journey I cannot logically attribute to anything reasonable, and so have me baffled, yet grateful. I can only conclude that they are a result of either sheer luck, a miracle, the work of the ancestors, possibly just the forces of the Universe at work, or a combination there of. Whichever it might be, they took their time on occurring and I hope that if you begin your own journey, you will encounter occurrences that will inspire you. If you find yourself already on the path, I hope that an occurrence, whatever it might be, will act as a catalyst for you to continue. …. Godspeed.

CHAPTER 1

CORAL'S FEAST

[1st Occurrence – Medicine Man's In-site]

"Coral, look your Grandpa Castillo has just arrived. Make sure you go and say hello."

The Medicine man / Spiritual person, Robert "Bob" Cervantes from the Jicarilla Reservation, and others in the ceremonial party were sitting in a circle with our family. Some attendees had come from the Jicarilla reservation, others were from different parts of Texas, as well as others who were local people. They came here to Alice, Texas in support of Coral on this very important time for the Apache people on March 15th – 18th, 2010. As we sat talking, I noticed the Medicine man kept staring at my father. After a about 30 minutes, I finally spoke up and asked Bob, "Why do you keep staring at my father?" He told me "Your father is a Native American man and has STRONG Native blood and a special person." {Appendix A: Occurrence #1} He and my father had never met before. I responded with "Yes, he is special he is my father." I also acknowledged that we know that his family was indigenous, however, we did not know of what Tribe or Nation. This acknowledgment of my father's presence to the Medicine man struck me profoundly.

My daughter's Feast/Sunrise/Coming of Age Ceremony was performed because we knew that on my mother's side of the family (Dorothy Ruiz), we were Lipan Apache. Through my maternal Great Grandparents, who raised my mother from a young child, and had

71

been taught some of the Apache ways. It was at that special spiritual event that I realized that I needed to continue with my father's ancestry.

The fact that my father's ancestry, to a point was unknown, at least to me, and the strong suggestion by the medicine man, sent me on a continued search to attempt to find out more. After Coral's ceremony, I got started right away working again on my father's side of the family ancestry. I had been able to previously trace back to my Great, Great, Grandfather Jose Pablo Castillo. {Table 1, pg.73}

I was able to confirm these through Oral History, Government records, Civil records, religious affiliated records, Ancestry.com, Birth and Death Certificates, News Articles, Scholarly published works and internet searches, which I also referred to while completing this project. [1-10] But then I hit a roadblock and discouragement set in. A few years went by and the thought of finding what Tribe or Nation my father's family came from was put on the backburner.

Table 1

The following is a direct linage from Thomas Castillo to Lipan Chief Castillo. *

Me – Thomas Castillo [1]

My Father – Reyes Castillo [2,3]

My Grand Father – Tomas Castillo [3,5,22]

My Great Grand Father – Trinidad Castillo [4,6]

My Great, Great, Grand Father – Jose Pablo Castillo [4,6,7,21]

MY Great, Great, Great, Grand Father – Chief Castillo [7]

*Note: According to one of my first cousins, research into the Castillo family linage took another cousin into Mexico to find the ancestry in the late 1970's. She said that through hearsay it was mentioned that Jose Pablo Castillo was an adopt as a child. Which could collaborate with the New Mexico census information and Tio Emilio's oral history. Also, through hearsay it was said that his father's first name could have been Esaias. Unfortunately, my cousin said that the notes on that ancestry were lost. After much research and time, I have not been able to confirm this name, and so therefor I only referred to Jose Pablo's father as Chief Castillo.

CHAPTER 2
IN THE BEGINNING

My father's Tribal or Nation affiliation had always been in the back of my mind, and I had a great desire ever since Coral's Ceremony to find out. I finally got the time to continue where I left off and was going to attempt again to find our Native ancestry on my father's side of the family. By this time my Grand Father Tomas had already crossed over to the spirit world, and I never got the chance to ask him about our lineage. [5]

This journey started in 1991 after I had started my educational career, finding my ancestors up to Jose Pablo Castillo. Hitting a roadblock after that I stepped away and did not revisit my research until I left High School athletic coaching in 2006. I then had more time on my hands to work on this. I wanted to find my father's ancestry on his father's side beyond my 3x-Great Grand Father Jose Pablo Castillo, which my father never spoke of, but my research this time was more fruitful, credited to perseverance.

I did remember that as a child my father would take us to Mexico to visit with my Grandfather Tomas, my namesake, and his brother (my father's uncle) "Tio Emilio". Well come to find out Tio Emilio was still alive and living in Nuevo Laredo, Tamaulipas, Mexico.

Next thing was to locate him and go for a visit. I asked my father if we could go and talk and visit Tio Emilio so I could ask about our ancestry. My father was hesitant at first, but after bugging him a few times he reluctantly agreed. So, on June 10th, 2006, my father, my son (Granet), and I went to Nuevo Laredo in search of Tio Emilio. When we got to Nuevo Laredo it didn't take too long to locate Tio Emilio, he was living in an old rundown apt/shack. It was off a dirt road and had chickens roaming free around us. We sat outside on an old wooden table with old rusty metal chairs under a tree on a hot summer day. I believe there was no air conditioning in the home, so it was more comfortable outside under a large shade tree and with a slight breeze. We talked for hours and had lunch and cool drinks, Aguas.

I had taken photos using a Motorola flip phone I had at the time. I have kept the phone throughout the years due to the photos that it contains but never got around to downloading them. My mistake was waiting too long, and as time passed, since then, I was not able to extract the photos from the old phone. I attempted to go to several computer/phone repair shops to no avail. I even contacted a couple of Nationally esteemed forensic computer/phone specialists, but they could not get the photos either, too much time had passed, and old technology had sealed the fate of the pictures. I still do have possession of the phone, however.

I distinctively remember that my brother and I, as children, would go with my father to "Mexico" to visit. I remember that my Tio Emilio was occasionally referred to as "Chief". I eventually found it kind of strange because in Mexico "Chief" was not used, "Jefe" was the usual word used. I always thought that Tio Emilio was referred to "Chief" because he was a police officer and that he was the "Chief of Police", the guy in charge of the police. But I came to find out all these years later that it was not the case.

All our conversations were in Spanish, and I was very grateful I understood it. Unfortunately, Granet didn't know much Spanish at that time and just listened to the conversations in a language not very familiar to him, though I know he picked up on some words, and phrases here and there and I translated some as the conversation went along.

The following is the jest of our conversations dealing with our ancestors; however, we would talk about various topics but always came back to family discussions time and again.

Through our conversations (oral history) I learned that we were indeed indigenous people. I found out that this information was never passed down to the children due to the concerns the family had of our families' identities being found out by others, especially the U.S. Army and U.S. Government. [7]

As Tio Emilio eventually told us about our family history, I could not tell, nor did I know, if my father was privy to any or all the oral history we were being told. My father would say nothing to add yet just sat silently and nodded his head as in agreement or understanding with what Tio Emilio told us.

I had taken a small notebook to take down notes on what might have been said. However, Tio Emilio told me not to write anything, he said "Just listen and remember". [7]

CHAPTER 3

TIO EMILIO SPEAKS

[2nd Occurrence – Chief in the Family]

Tio Emilio started by saying that we were descendants of "Chief Castillo"! {Appendix A: Occurrence #2}. [7] He then showed us a ring he was wearing of an Indian with a feather bonnet. I had taken a picture of him and the ring, but again I was not able to get that picture from my phone. However, I distinctively remembered how it looked and eventually bought a very similar ring for myself. [7]

Well as you can imagine that sparked my interest immediately. For the rest of the oral history being told to us, all I could do was keep thinking to myself, how was I going to verify this. With a mathematical background I felt the need to have to prove this oral history to be accepted as facts, or at least to gather convincing evidence.

Tio Emilio told us that Chief Castillo had been killed by the U.S. Army when they ambushed him and some companions in Tejas. He said that some of the companions were able to get away. He went on to say that it was not known what had happened to Chief Castillo's body, for when the companions who had escaped the ambush came back to get the body, it was gone. Tio Emilio stated that "since that day the Castillo's were wary of the U.S. Govt and the U.S. Army". [7] According to Tio Emilio when the word got back to Chief Castillo's family the family clan disbursed. Chief Castillo's young son (Jose "Pablo" Castillo) was then sent far away with a relative, (possibly an uncle – Anastacio Castillo), to where they hoped the U.S. Army,

Mexican Army, and Texas Rangers would not find him in New Mexico. [8a-8f] He further added that that was the end of our families' "Indian ways", "Aye se acavo nuestras maneras indigena." [7] This made a lot more sense once I completed Part I of this project. Tio Emilio said that Jose Pablo Castillo was raised and assimilated into the new way of life and culture. Never again to use the old ways of his people for his protection, however he always knew of his father's fate and knew that the family was originally from Texas. When Chief Castillo's son (now referred to by family as Chief Jose Pablo Castillo) was old enough he and Castillo family members found their way into Mexico, (Most likely due to the beginning of the Civil War, Indian Wars, and avoiding the scalp bounties being offered.[8a- 8c, 22]), and ended up in Southern Nuevo Leon near San Luis Potosi, around Dr. Arroyo. [9,10] Most likely the San Luis Potosi area was chosen since there had historically been Lipan Apacherias in that vicinity and quite possibly since it was also Peyote territory. [12] From there the family moved to La Lajita and Venado, Nuevo Leon, which is in close proximity to Dr. Arroyo, and the clan was reformed.

[map 9 Mexico and South Texas Towns pg.79]

78

Texas

Coahuila

Corpus Christi

Alice

Laredo

Trinidad Lake

Nuevo Leon

Gulf

of

Mexico

La Lajita

Tamaulipas

Doctor Arroyo

Venado

Zacatecas

Villa de Arista

San Luis Potosi

San Luis Potosi

South Texas and North
Eastern Mexico Towns
Prepared by: T. Castillo
2025

Map 9

It is important to note that from this point forward, the "title" of "Chief" was basically use by the family to designate the head of the family, and not as a Native American leader of a band or tribe as was used to designate "Chief Castillo", as is in several citations. [Appendix H][11a-11f] This is because by this point in time the Tribal collect was disbursed due to pressures from various Governments, Diseases, and competing Tribes. [8d-8f]

Tio Emilio continued saying that the family (clan) came back to Texas from Dr. Arroyo (the area), Nuevo Leon, Mexico. This occurred after the death of Chief Jose Pablo Castillo [13] for several reasons. One was to look for work as migrant workers. Another was to get away from the Mexican "political" revolution. [14] Yet another was Trinidad Castillo's (now the family Chief) desire to return to the family clan's homelands. [15]

While the Castillo Family Clan was in Texas, (at a ranch near Waelder, Texas) again, Trinidad Castillo's eldest son (Tomas Castillo) had a son and a younger daughter, Reyes Castillo and Rosa Castillo, my father, and my aunt. (Both now deceased.) [3, 16, 17] Throughout Tio Emilio's oral history of the family he never revealed what Tribe or Nation the family belonged to. I don't know why. When I asked (interrupting him about it) he just pointed at me, shook his head, and said "escuheme", (Just listen) I never did get an answer to the question. I have now gotten the impression that he might have felt that it would have been too much information which could be harmful.

My father had already told me of the time when the family clan was in Texas, and that the family Chief, Trinidad, had been killed by the U.S. Army in Gonzales County near Waelder, Texas on March 2nd, 1937. The family men were returning by foot from working on the fields when a large U.S. Army truck steered off the road and went towards the men. Both said that Trinidad was able to warn and push his sons out of the way of the truck, however the U.S. Army truck struck and killed him. [4, 18] And so, now Chief Castillo and his grandson Trinidad, were both killed at the hands of the U.S. Army. When my father requested, in mid-1970's, for the incident from the U.S. Army they refused to release it to his attorney using the statute of limitations excuse. My father did not pursue the request any further. However, the State of Texas has no statute of limitations on manslaughter.

After all the years of the Castillo's being wary of the U.S. Government and U.S. Army this "incident" just worked to exacerbate the ill feelings of being a "marked" family. We can now see that the Castillo Clan would have bases for this claim, since we know now that that the U.S. government knew of Chief Castillo and even distinguished him as a "Man of Consequence"! [28a – 28g, 30]
Soon after the murder of family Chief Trinidad Castillo by a U.S. Army truck, Tomas Castillo (the new Family Chief) moved most of the clan back to Mexico settling at or near the border town of Nuevo Laredo, Tamp. Mexico. They settled in this part of Mexico because the Mexican government was at the time distributing land in that area at very inexpensive prices. [19] Now the clan vowed never to live in the U.S. again. However eventually some of the men returned to the U.S. as migrant workers.

Another "incident" Tio Emilio told us about, that occurred which added to the wariness of the clan towards the U.S., happened right after Tio Emilio's last migrant worker job in the 1950's. It transpired when Tio Emilio was returning to Nuevo Laredo. Prior to returning Tio Emilio had purchased, with his earned and saved money, a new Cadillac Automobile. Upon reaching the Border on the U.S. side he was questioned by the white U.S. Government Officials, as to how a person such as himself, (Brown and indigenous) was able to have a fine car as that. Tio Emilio said he tried to explain that he had earned and saved his money for it but to no avail. His new car was impounded, and he realized that he was about to be arrested (for an unknown reason) because he understood English and overheard the Officers talking and moving towards him. At that point he ran towards the border and crossed into Mexico, never to return to the U.S. and his new car, as he put it, stolen by the U.S. Government Tio Emilio continued with the oral history saying that my Grandfather Tomas was the head of the clan (Being the eldest), the Chief. He received that distinction after Trinidad was killed by the Army Truck. He said that my grandfather lost his distinction of family Chief when the family clan returned to Nuevo Laredo and pooled their monies to purchase the land offered by the Mexican Government. My Grandfather took the monies and purchased instead some property from a private landowner and was swindled with a deal that was corrupt. The Clan just received a small lot which was big enough for just a few people to live in and not to cultivate. The Family lost confidence in my grandfather and turned to his younger brother Emilio as the family "Chief".

I then knew why Tio Emilio was referred to as "Chief". All the while I believed he was called "Chief", as I mentioned earlier, thinking he was the "Chief of Police."

Before leaving that day Tio Emilio broke down and cried, I believe that it was due to his recollection of the family Clans history which was bottled up inside him. It seemed like a great relief to him to disclose all this information about our Castillo Clan. He also told my father that he was the now the new "Chief" since it was my grandfather's right, and it should be passed down to his son (my father).

I got a feeling that Tio Emilio's sons and immediate family to this day had not been told the family history. I felt that he cried because the family clan was now all gone.

CHAPTER 4

RE-CONNECTION

(3rd Occurrence – My Fathers Trek)

I don't know if Tio Emilio would approve of me putting this on paper, but I hope he will be OK with it. Tio Emilio crossed over to the spirit word soon after he shared with my father, me, and my son our oral history of the Castillo clan. [20]

My father, Reyes Castillo, seemed to not understand, or know what to make of this new title being bestowed upon him. Most likely because there was no longer a "Castillo Family Clan". Also, my father was removed from the Castillo family clan at a young age.

My father and aunt were essentially raised by my grandmother Maximina Serrato Gomez (Middle and Last names are maiden names). At a young age my father, about 8 years old, and my aunt Rosa were taken away from the Castillo family clan in Texas and moved to Villa de Artista, San Louis Potosi, Mexico where my grandmother Maximina was born and where her family was. Once there her "well to do" family did not make my grandmother feel comfortable, (since she had run away with an Indio while in Texas, and had "dos inditos", both my father and my aunt had dark complexions), so she took the children to live in Monterrey, Nuevo Leon, Mexico. Eventually Maximina remarried to what my father called "a Gachupin", Alvaro Martinez. It was this stepfather, Martinez, of my father who was the catalyst for my father's entrepreneurship ways.

My father had told me of how he never was able to see his real father as a child since he was raised in Monterrey, Nuevo Leon, Mexico and his father was now living in Nuevo Laredo, Tamaulipas, Mexico and was never taken to go visit him. He told me on various occasions that at 13 years old he left Monterrey on foot in search of his father, Tomas. He said that it took him 2 days to get to Nuevo Laredo. He said that he ate some provisions he had taken with him and drank water from some streams along the way.[map 10 Monterrey NL, MX to Nuevo Laredo Tamps. MX pg.86] He said that he remembered that when he swallowed the water at one place, he was very thirsty and just drank and could feel "little things squirming around as he drank!" He made it to Nuevo Laredo and did not know where to go to look for his father. He would ask people if they knew his father, but to no avail. At one point he saw a man on a bicycle selling menudo out of a pot but didn't get the chance to ask him.

He was eager to find his father because he was told back in Monterrey that his father was the owner of a fine restaurant, and that he was very hungry and wanted to find him to hopefully get something to eat. As the night came and he, having no luck, looked for a place to sleep for the night. He said that he was very tired and so he laid down on the dirt sidewalk and fell asleep when the owner of a bar nearby saw him and asked why he was sleeping there. My father told him the story, and the gentleman did not know his father, or any restaurant owned by a Castillo. The owner of the bar told him he could come in and sleep in his bar for the night and feed him if he would sweep and clean-up in the morning. My father agreed. After he finished cleaning, he continued his quest to find his father. He finally spoke to someone who knew Tomas Castillo and got directions to his place. He went to his father's place and found his father. He was the man on the bicycle selling menudo out of a pot.

The place was on the outskirts of the town, a Jacal with three walls and a roof, not quite what he was expecting. But he said he was very happy to have finally found and met his father. He said that they treated him very well and that he was very happy. After that he was sent (by bus) back to Monterrey. As he got older, he would go to visit his father often. I do remember the many trips we took when my father would take my brother and I, as children, to go see my "Welo Tomas" in Nuevo Laredo.

I consider this another {Occurrence #3}. A 13-year-old boy had such a strong desire to connect (reconnect) with his father, and that side of his family, that it would possess him to take a long-distance journey on foot with possible unknowns and danger.

CHAPTER 5
THE LINK

Eventually, after my father's service with the U.S. Army, (Drafted – I don't believe my father knew of the total Castillo Clan history with the U.S. Army and Government at this point), my father went to Corpus Christi, Texas where my grandmother Maximina (now remarried to Ismael Gonzalez) and Tia Rosa, his sister, were living. Soon after, my father met and married my mother (Dorothy Ruiz) and had two sons, (Reyes Castillo Jr. and myself, Thomas Castillo). It is worth noting that at some point prior to marring my mother, he had a daughter, Diane Castillo, with his first wife Elena Cordoba in Mexico. After a divorce from Dorothy my father married Elvia Garcia of Nuevo Laredo, Tamaulipas, Mexico. and had two daughters, my lovely stepsisters, (Elvia Lorena Castillo and Nieves Castillo).

Approximately 7 years had gone by since we had gotten the oral history from Tio Emilio, and I had worked on this project off and on, making little progress. During that time, thanks to Tio Emilio's oral history of Chief Castillo sending his son to New Mexico, I was finally able to track the linage further back of Jose Pablo Castillo, who was listed as a "Servant Indian" in the 1860 New Mexico census. [21] On the census Jose Pablo Castillo is listed as living with the "Castillo" household, however he is listed as an **Indian servant** and not as a relative, (that is either a son, daughter, cousin, etc.). To my delight I had found the son of the murdered "Chief Castillo". Several things led me to that conclusion.:

1) According to Tio Emilio's Oral history "Chief Castillo's son was sent to New Mexico to live with relatives. [7]

2) Jose Pablo Castillo was listed in the New Mexico 1860 census, chronologically correct. [21]

3) Jose Pablo Castillo was listed as an INDIAN SERVANT, and not as an immediate family member. [21]

4) Jose Pablo was listed as a "Castillo". [21]

5) A **direct documented lineage** has been made from myself to Jose Pablo Castillo. [1, 3, 4,5,6,9,21,23]

6) Being Listed as an INDIAN SERVANT shows that Jose Pablo Castillo was classified as a NATIVE AMERICAN and **not** classified as 'White" like the rest of the household members. [21]

7) <u>Anastacio Castillo</u> was listed as head of household in N.M. USA Census with Jose Pablo Castillo, not as his father [21] I believe Anastacio was most likely an Uncle to Jose Pablo, although no documentation for this has been found yet.

8) <u>Anastacia Castillo</u> was listed as a family member (Mother) of Jose Pablo Castillo in Mexico in 1 document,[9] then upon Jose Pablo Castillo's death it is documented that his parents were "Unknown". [13] Here, again, it's viable that Anastacia could have been the mother to Jose Pablo and sister or sister-in-law to Anastacio. Therefor Anastacia, would have also been Lipan and wife to Chief Castillo. But no other documentation to further confirm Anastacia relationship to Anastacio or Jose Pablo has been found at the time of this project.

The 6th point is very significant because this was during the time when it was not good to be an Indian. During this time-period Indians were still looked upon as best low-class citizens, and/or "unmitigated nuisance" to the community, especially the Lipan. [24g] There was still a bounty for Indian scalps, (which could be redeemed by just about anyone). [23a, 23b] As well as, at this time, the U.S. Army, the Mexican Army, and the Texas Rangers were all still patrolling and killing Indians since some Lipan Apache refused to be contained on reservations or missions at that time. [8a-8f] So, listing Jose Pablo Castillo as an "Indian Servant" could help to distant him from the rest of the household in New Mexico and therefor keeping them somewhat safe from the aforementioned military actions. [8a-8f,23a,23b,24a-24h]

The big and only issue left was finding "Chief Castillo" that Tio Emilio had referred to. After many years of searching on and off, I was not able to find a "Chief Castillo" in any Documents, Publications, Reports, etc. Except for a Tonkawa Chief Castil, whom was often mis-labeled as "Castillo", however Chief Castil's death was recorded well after Chief Castillo's death, as I would later find out. [27a-27c] Feeling discouraged I just about gave up, again, thinking that this was an impossible task, and too much time was already spent on it without any further success.

Though my search for "Chief Castillo" I had found Native American "Castillo's" as part of the Lipan Apache Tribe. There is reference to "Castillo's" listed as Lipan Apache tribal members, Headmen, and leaders in several reports and documented in publications, but no "Chief Castillo" [11a-11f] I had always wondered if any of these Castillo's listed as Lipan Apache could be ancestors of our family clan. This was interesting to me because my mother, from her maternal side, was Lipan Apache. However, I could not find no affirmative documentation throughout all those years on "Chief Castillo".

I had always wondered about the Lipans', "Castillo's". They were from Texas, during the period, which was comparable to Chief Castillo's, but nothing definitive could be found to connect our ancestor "Castillo Indian Servant" in New Mexico or "Chief Castillo" to any of these documented Lipan Castillo's. [11a-11f]

So, in essence there was a big disconnect between the "Castillo Indian Servant" in New Mexico and the Oral History of "Chief Castillo" due to not finding any viable documentation on a "Chief Castillo".

CHAPTER 6

UNEXPECTED DISCOVERY

(4th Occurrence – Article at C.C. Library)

More years passed and hope was just about lost that a connection between the oral history of a Chief Castillo and the Castillo Indian Servant would ever be made. Then, one day after my daughter's ceremony, in the fall of 2013 my wife (Diana) and I took our youngest son (Stone) to the Corpus Christi La Retama Public Library for some work he needed to do for a Scouting project. While at the Library I found myself looking around killing time, looking at art and reading articles which were scattered throughout concerning the history of Corpus Christi and the surrounding areas. Some of the articles were current and some were from historical times. This is when I stumbled upon, and to my complete surprise, a totally unexpected and not in the least looking for it, an old historical article concerning an Indian raid near the town of San Diego, Texas on July 11th of 1854, in which the U.S. Army had conducted a raid to kill area Indians. {Appendix A: Occurrence #4} This article was written only because it stated, and headlined, about a U.S. Army Captain Michael E. Van Beuren being killed during the fight. As I got to the end of the article, which in and of its self, surprises me, that I read it all, it was mentioned that a Lipan Apache scout, that was with the U.S. Army, had said that one of the Indians killed was "Chief Castillo", the scout saying that Chief Castillo was "much revered by his people" leader of the Comanches. **Comanches!?** [27a – 27g]

I was so excited and knew that I would now, with this new information, be able to get back to the Castillo Clan research. I felt

that this was a very definitive documentation that Chief Castillo
existed during a period that was comparable to that of the Chief
Castillo's Clan oral history. In May of 2015, I took it upon myself to
contact the Historical Center of the Comanche Nation in Lawton
Oklahoma to confirm with them the existence of a Comanche Chief
"Castillo". I spoke to Martina Minthorn, the Cultural Preservation
Officer of the Comanche Nation. She said that they were not aware
of any historical Chief Castillo of the Comanche Nation. She said
that she could just about definitively say that there was never a
Comanche Chief Castillo since most Comanche Chiefs had "natural
type names". She said that except for a couple of well-known chiefs
all the rest were names which referred to animals or nature. She said
some publications mention Comanche Chief names in Spanish
however these were translations from the Comanche language. She
did say that she would investigate it and contact me if she ever found
anything. I did not hear back from her and again I was stuck with
lack of information for a short time. Fast forward to 2022, 7 years
later, I was now the counterpart to Martina as the Lipan Apache
Cultural Preservation Officer for the Lipan Apache Tribe of Texas.
We got to meet at a symposium that was put on by Angelo State

University. The symposium took place at Paint Rock, Texas to
discuss and examine rock art, petroglyph, and pictographs there. I
had asked her if she ever came across any information concerning
the Comanche Chief Castillo, to which she said she did not, and most
likely there was never a Comanche Chief Castillo.
I then decided to do my own research on Comanche Chief names to
verify and confirm what Martina had reiterated to me.[29]
 {Appendix C}

CHAPTER 7
PRESIDENT OF THE UNITED STATES

(5th Occurrence – Message from President of U.S.)

Later that year (2015) I came across a book by Sherry Robinson which was published in 2013, "I Fought a Good Fight: A history of the Lipan Apache". While reading and studying the book I noted the following: that the U.S. Army in the spring of 1854 had located and attacked some Lipan at Lake Trinidad about forty miles southwest of Fort Merrill at Dinero, Texas. (About 10 miles from San Diego, Texas as a crow flies.) [Map 7 Direction of U.S. Army Travel Pg.45] This source also stated that a U.S. Army detachment also chased the same Lipan group from Trinidad Lake to Arroyo Baluarte who were led by "Chief Castillo"! Documented proof that a possible Lipan Chief Castillo existed!

With this came one of the most exciting leads at the same time. {Appendices A and F: Occurrence #5} It happened that I came across an internet search engine result, that I had never seen before in the almost 10 years of searching for "Chief Castillo". Out of nowhere in cyber space a hit on a search which completely solidified that there was a Lipan Chief Castillo. It had come from a report of the U.S. Department of Defense in Texas by General P. Smith which was included in the "Message from the President of the United States to the Second session of the 33rd Congress" It included statements concerning "Lipan Chief Castillo"!

I had concluded that a Chief "Castillo" was not a viable Comanche name since the Comanche used "animal" and/or "nature" type names. Castillo is a name which is a Spanish name and one that translates to Castle, not very natural. However, I would later discover that "Castillo" was actually and converted nature type of name. {Appendix E}

So, by processing and using reasonable logic of the following,

1) There was a very small probability that the "Chief Castillo" killed by the U.S. Army near San Diego, Texas. was a Comanche Chief. [28]

2) The Castillo Clan oral history states of a killed "Chief Castillo" in Texas. [7]

3) The fact was that it was a **Lipan** scout who identified Chief Castillo and as a "much revered" leader, which matches the message from the President of the United States which proclaims that Lipan "Chief Castillo was a man of Consequence" [27c, 29]

4) The fact that during that time in history it was common for the Lipan and Comanche to often blame each other and redirect negative and positive events, to and from each other, when reporting to the U.S. Army and Government. [30] {Appendix D}

5) The fact of documented Lipan "Castillo's" existed as Tribal Members, Leaders, and headmen. [11a-11f]

6) The fact that most Comanche Chiefs did not have Spanish names, however some names were "translated" into Spanish. [28] {Appendix C}

7) The Lipan name "Castillo" most likely come from "Roque". There was a Chief Roque for the Lipan Apaches. {Appendix E}

8) The fact that within a few weeks the U.S. army had been in the same vicinity **after Chief Castillo** at Lake Trinidad, (just south of Ben Bolt near San Diego, Texas; then at Arroyo Baluarte) [31] [map 3]

9) Lipan were recorded being and living within the same time-period and vicinity. [33 – 40] {Appendix G}

10) Within that time-period the Comanche were recorded as being in areas for away from the San Diego, Texas area. [41 – 46]

11) Through DNA it has been shown that I (Thomas Castillo) have matching DNA to other Lipan Apache Tribal People using Ancestry.com/GEDMatch.com,

a conclusion can be drawn that the Lipan scout for the U.S. Army, the U.S Army itself, or other reporting could have falsified or misreported the information given, that Chief Castillo was Comanche, whom should of instead have been reported as Lipan as in other reports. [31] However, if this information was falsified, a motive would be needed to explain why. There are four very strong reasons that can answer this question.

1) It would put the blame on the Comanche (correctly) for raids that had occurred in Laredo, Texas, which lead to the U.S. Army's need to locate the falsely blamed Lipans, as well as blaming the Comanche for coming to South Texas away from their designated lands at the time. [30] {Appendix D}

2) The scouts decreasing, or eliminating, the possibility of having more search parties who would have been put together to find and kill more of his own tribal people, the Lipan Apache. [24a-24h]

3) The U.S. army having picked up the wrong trail and needed to save face. [27b]

4) Since Lipan were seen as a menace and needed to be exterminated, it might have been more "prestigious" for the news reports to have been changed to reflect that Captain Van Buren had been killed by a Comanche. [24g]

Adding to this evidence is the fact the Lipan Scout was adamant enough to say in his report that Chief Castillo was a "much revered leader". This poses a question, "Why?", why would a Lipan Apache Scout be referring to a Comanche Leader as a "much revered leader"? When during those times there was a lot of animosity between the Comanche and the Lipan Apache. [50] If indeed Chief Castillo was much revered, and much revered by the **Lipan Apache**, then the Lipan Scout would have had basis for this part of his statement, which he felt was important enough to be included in the report. Also, how would a U.S Army Lipan Scout have known a Comanche Chief and the Comanche tribal people enough to make a statement like this?

Yet another piece of evidence is the fact that the Lipan Apache would go into Mexico, a map shows the routes the Lipan, and other tribes, mainly Comanche, would use to go into Mexico. Most routes are notorious Comanche raiding routes; however, these same paths were used prior to the Comanche by the Lipan, until the Lipan were forced from them, and the Lipan started to enter Mexico further South and East. [23b, 32] Also, some routes coming from the west did extended onto the eastern routs. [map 11 Western Lipan and Comanche Trails pg.99 ; map 12 Eastern Lipan and Comanche Trails pg. 100]

Interestingly enough, one of the locations in Mexico that the Lipan would go to using these routes, was an area **exactly** in the vicinity of Dr. Arroyo, and La Lajita, NL., Mexico, the area where the Castillo's settled when in Mexico, near San Luis Potosi. [map 12 Eastern Lipan and Comanche Trails pg.100] Also, several accounts places Lipan in the San Luis Potosi vicinity, were the Castillo's were located at one point. [47,48]

After evaluating all this data gathered through years of research and showing an extremely high degree of correlation between the Castillo clan oral history and the documents discovered, I feel that not only is there an exceptional high probability, but also gives way to a very strong argument and great certainty, that the "Chief Castillo" who was killed by the U.S. Army near San Diego, Texas on

July 11th, 1854 was in reality a Lipan Apache Chief. The "Chief Castillo", referred to by Emilio Castillo in his oral history, as well as Sherri Robinson, and in Messages from President of U.S. to Congress all being one in the same. [24g, 29]

For Lipan Tribal distinction, I believe that using Agua Dulce, TX [54] as a last reference point for Chief Castillo's group encampment, and the fact that the Clan returned to Gonzales County, then on to the Border to Nuevo Laredo it can be established that the Castillo Clan came from the ancestral Lipan Sun Otter Clan.[25] [map 6 Lipan Band Territories pg. 33] This can also be evidenced by the missing Chief succession in the Sun Otter Band as listed in Nancy McGown-Minor's book "The Light Gray People" on page 106. There is a "gap" in the "Sun Otter extended family groups ca. 1800:", between (4) Chief Moreno (The Dark One, aka Tuclax-yelt'), (1791-1833) and (s) Chief Magoosh – (1850-1900).[53] This gap should be filled by Chief Castillo.

I hope you found this journey enlightening enough to start, or continue, your path of ancestry. Some simple advice I would like to share, keep an eye and ear out, for you never know when you will receive an "occurrence" that may cross your path. If you are just starting on your ancestral journey, you must prepare yourself, this will be a marathon....not a sprint.

The direct descendants and immediate family members as discovered from Lipan Chief Castillo to Thomas Castillo is as follows: [Table 2]

Table 2
Direct Decedents of Chief Castillo to Thomas R. Castillo and immediate Family Members:

Chief Castillo: My Great, Great, Great Grandfather (Anastacia?): Child –Jose Pablo Castillo

Jose Pablo Castillo** : My Great, Great, Grandfathers children (Ysidra Lira): Teresa Castillo, Jose del Changuito Trinidad Castillo, Nicandro de el Teposan Castillo, Jose Tomas Castillo, Jose E. Castillo, Longino Castillo

Trinidad Castillo : My Great Grandfathers children (Mariana Quinones) Tomas Castillo, Jose (Joe) Castillo, Nicandro Castillo, Pablo Castillo, Emilio Castillo, Clemente Castillo, Frank Castillo, Jesus Maria Castillo, Bernardo Castillo, Antonio Castillo, Jose Remedios Castillo

Tomas Q. Castillo : My Grandfathers Children (Maximina Serrato): Reyes
S. Castillo, Rosa Castillo; (Petra Rodriguez): Francisca Castillo

Reyes S. Castillo : My Fathers Children– (Elena Cordoba) Diane Castillo; (Dorothy Ruiz) Reyes Castillo Jr., Thomas Castillo; (Elvia Garcia) Elvia L. Castillo, Nieves Castillo

Thomas R. Castillo : My Children (Diana M. Romero): Granet Castillo [Longbow], Coral Castillo [Morning Star], Stone Castillo [Silent Hawk]

**Note: Interestingly enough, it was found that two of Jose Pablo Castillo's, (Chief Castillo's son), children were given what seem to be Indigenous type names….El Teposan, and El Changuito as legal description. A third, son of Trinidad Castillo, could have also been given an Indigenous name of "Remedios" which could be argued that it could be a biblical name referring to the Virgin Mary. However, that name was usually reserved for a Female name. The Native name could have referred to "Healer".

Also, it is just as impressive that Jose Pablo Castillo named one of his children Trinidad, the name of the Lake his father was killed at.

Equally important to notice are all the "Jose" Prefix names. These were not used much, mostly dropped as second name was used to identify the person.

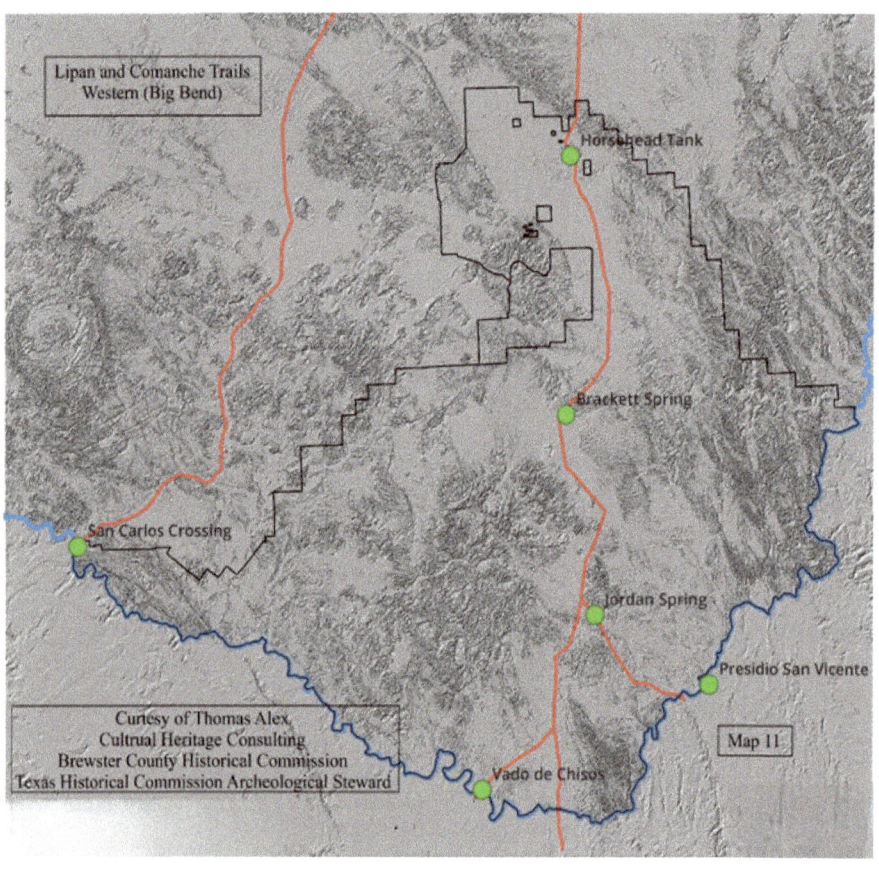

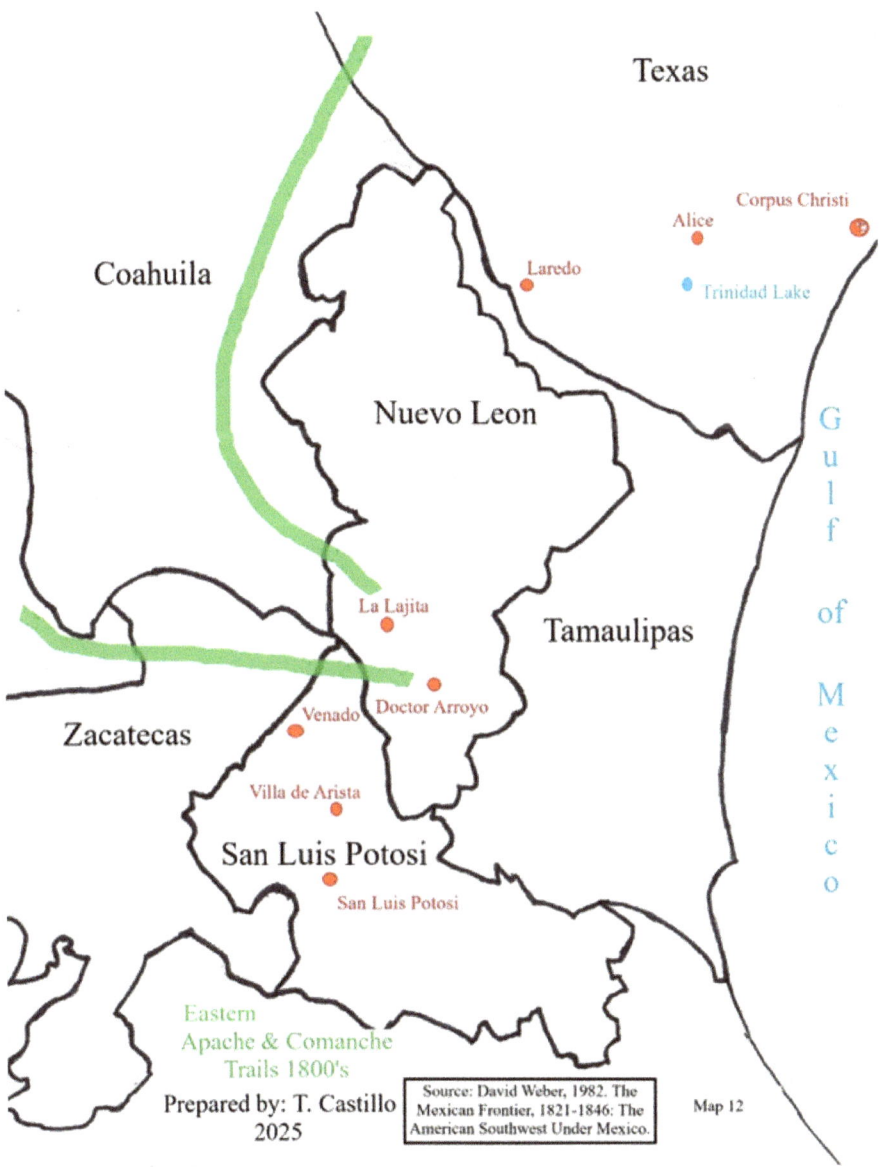

Texas

Coahuila

Corpus Christi

Alice

Laredo

Trinidad Lake

Nuevo Leon

G
u
l
f

of

M
e
x
i
c
o

La Lajita

Tamaulipas

Venado   Doctor Arroyo

Zacatecas

Villa de Arista

San Luis Potosi

San Luis Potosi

Eastern
Apache & Comanche
Trails 1800's

Prepared by: T. Castillo
2025

Source: David Weber, 1982. The
Mexican Frontier, 1821-1846: The
American Southwest Under Mexico.

Map 12

Final Words

I would like to finish by mentioning that this quest was rekindled at my daughter's (Coral Castillo) ceremony, thanks to Bob the Medicine man, which was held at the Jim Wells County Fairgrounds, and unbeknownst at the time, is Approx. 10 mi. from Lake Trinidad where her GGGG Grandfather, Chief Castillo was murdered.

"Let us not allow those that wish us gone to manipulate our time, rather we should use our limited resources and energy to bring back our people by enriching and strengthening them with the ways of our Ancestors"

-Tom BearClaw Castillo

"The Lipan must come back together. It will be our own divisions and colonial egos that will destroy us, something governments have never been able to do."

-Tom BearClaw Castillo

Appendix A
Explanations to "Occurrences"

Some things just can't be explained using logic or reason. These things, however, can play a significant role in your navigation to understand and gather insight into the broader picture of your work. The following is a list of "occurrences" that I feel were major contributors to accomplishing this project and without could have led to a void in the Castillo ancestral history.

Occurrence 1: Medicine man insight – Without doubt this left a profound kindling in me which did not take much to ignite and to continue my journey in finding the Tribe which my ancestors belonged to. I took the wisdom and recognition of our Medicine Man very seriously. This intuition identification felt to me like it had come in from left field. I was certainly not expecting anything like this which I would indulge in. I believe the Medicine Man, whether knowingly or not, contributed this information, through some force, to somehow challenge me to continue my work.

Occurrence 2: Chief in the family – When my father, son and I went to visit my great uncle at Nuevo Laredo,Tamaulipas, Mexico I was hoping to just hear information about our family's history. Then Tio Emilio revealed that there was a Chief in the family. I was absolutely flabbergasted when I learned we had a Chief in the family. This again immediately sparked an interest and had given me not only a new lead, but an incredible sense of pride. I think back and wonder what if I had not been so adamant towards my work and had not insisted on going to see Tio Emilio, this whole historical information concerning the Castillo's' could have been lost forever.

Occurrence 3: My father's Trek – Although chronologically this happened before the others, I feel this was a major contributor to the discovery of the Castillo's history. Not only did this evidence show a strong will, perseverance and an acute desire to accomplish, but also displayed an unexplainable urge to reconnect. My father's trek from Monterrey, Nuevo Leon, Mexico to Nuevo Laredo, Tamaulipas Mexico, on foot no less, I feel was an extraordinary adventure and did it at age 13! Total Km/Miles traveled – 230Km/140mi. Had my father not taken this journey his ties to the Castillo side of the family could have been hidden away in the unrefined annals of history.

Occurrence 4: Article at C.C. Library – To this day if find it bewildering that after many years of research and study, I just happened to come across the news article mentioning Chief Castillo by chance. To add, knowing myself and my impatience, I am amazed that I lasted to read to the end of the lengthy article. It was at the very end, like a footnote that the article mentioned Chief Castillo. Ordinarily I would have skimmed the beginning of the article and moved on. I don't know what possessed me to continue reading till the end, but it paid off immensely. I can't explain what force, if any, gravitated me to the article or why I read through it to the end, but it played an important role in this project.

Occurrence 5: Message from the President of U.S. – Another unexplainable yet exciting find was the "Message from the President of the U.S. to the Second Session of the 33rd Congress". Within the Message was a report from the Department of Defense in Corpus

Christi, TX. It was a report made by General P. Smith, commander of the Defense Department in Texas. After years of searching the internet for a lead to Chief Castillo, Sherry Robinson and the cyber algorithms finally awarded me with a piece of evidence that came directly from the President of the United States! I have trouble even now with a search that would lead me back to this discovery. This was an incredible find, as it mentioned that "Lipan Chief Castillo was a man of consequence"

It was this, (Occurrence #5), discovery that led me to Part I of this book (Lipan Chief Castillo – 1854). After this discovery I began digging into Lipan Chief Castillo, now the more I searched the more that came to light. Bits and pieces were scattered throughout a lot of sources that I came across. Many of the pieces I had come across over and over yet not understanding each individually. But then I realized that they were all connected. I needed to piece it all together to get chronological and logical historical accounts of the last days of Chief Castillo.

If not for the kindness of Sherry Robinson's work, and the cyber gods, this element in history might have never been known. And so, my point for, and, throughout all this concerning "occurrences" would be, don't give up. If you need to take a break then take some time off, just keep a watchful eye, opened ears and stay vigilant, for "occurrences" may happen at any time.

Appendix B

Oral history of Emilio Castillo, (2006): Interview – Nuevo Laredo,Tamaulipas, Mexico.
By Thomas Castillo – Deposition (2023)

Deposition by Thomas R. Castillo

On the oral history of the Castillo Clan as told to me by Emilio (Emilio) Castillo on June 10th, 2006, in Nuevo Laredo, Tamaulipas, Mexico.

All the accounts were in Spanish; I have translated these accounts into English.

I asked Tio Emilio if he was aware of any Indians in our family. He gave me a stern look and said, "Bueno". [OK]

Tio Emilio began by showing us his Indian Chief Ring he was wearing.

"Este lo a tenido por munchos anos." [He said that he had had that ring for a long time, years.]

"Este no me lo quitaron." [This one they did not take away.] I asked why he wore that particular ring.

"Es para recordar que nosotros somos indios y que teniamos un Jefe Castillo en la familia." [This is to remind me that we are Indian and that we had a Chief Castillo in the family.]

I was ready to record the oral history on a pad that I had taken with me, but he told me, "No escribes nada, nomas escuchame y recurdate." [Don't write anything, just listen and remember.]

"Nuestra hente les fue muy mal. Eranos indios y nos trataron muy mal. Mataron a unos, les cortaron el cabello con cuero a ortros, querian que peliamos en sus gurreras, nos dieron enfermedades, y eso fue por todos lados, los Federales, Mexicanos, los Tejanos, y los Americanos."

[It went bad for our people. We were Indians and so they treated us badly. They would kill some, they would scalp some, they would want us to fight in their wars, they would give us diseases, and it was from all sides, the Mexican Army, the Texans, and the American Army.

I asked him to tell me about Chief Castillo that he wore the ring for.

"Mi hente me contaron que un dia los Americanos atacaron y mataron a el Jefe Castillo y unos companieros, pero otros se escaparon, fue in el sur de Tejas."

[My family told me that one day the American Army attacked and killed Chief Castillo and some of the men with him, but others escaped this was in South Texas.]

"Quando eso paso los que se escaparon regressaron a recojer el cuerpo del el Jefe Castillo y los otros pero no estavan aye."

[After this happened the ones that escaped returned to get the bodies of Chief Castillo and the others, but they were not there".]

"Desde ese dia los Castillos no teinen confianza a los Americanos. "

[Since that day the Castillos have no trust in the American Army.]

"Quando le dieron cuenta a la jente de lo que paso, se llevaron a el hijo, Jose Pablo, de el Jefe Castillo a viver in Nuevo Mexico para que los Americanos no lo encontraran. Y eso es quando se acabo nuestro indianidad. Y la jente se fue a sus differentes rumbos.

[When the family found out about the attack, they took Chief Castillo's son, Jose Pablo, to go live in New Mexico to get away from the American Army. And that was when our Indianness ended. And the people went their separate ways.]

"Jose Pablo se aumento vivendo como jente civil, pero de servante. Luego se vino a viver en Mexico, a Venado, cuando los Americanos querian que el peleara con ellos en la gurra Civil de los Estados Unidos."

[Jose Pablo was raised and assimilated, but as a servant. Then he went to, Venado, San Luis Potosi, Mexico when the American Army wanted him to fight for them in the United States Civil war.]

"En Venado nacio mi padre Trinidad, y mi abulo Jefe Jose Pablo fallecio in Matehuala."

[My father was born in Venado, San Luis Potosi, Mexico and my grandfather Chief Jose Pablo died in Matehuala.]

"Yo naci en La Lajita, Nuevo Leon, como 30 minutos de Dr Arroyo. Aye en La Lajita estava la familia.

Luego mi padre ahora el jefe movio toda la family patras para Tejas por rason de la politica y para a yar tabajo con buien pago, a Wealder."

[I was born in La Lajita, Nuevo Leon Mexico about 30 minutes from Dr Arroyo. There at La Lajita was the Family. Then my father now the Chief moved all the family back to Texas due to the Mexican political problems and to find better paying jobs, to Wealder]

I interrupted him once to ask if he knew what tribe we belonged to, he just shook his head and said "Escuha me", [Listen to me].

"Regresamos a Mexico des pues que el ejercito Americano, estaves, mataron a mi padre, el Jefe Trinidad. Un dia los hombres de la family estaban andando para tras de trabajando en los campos cuando un camion de el ejercito Americano fue y estrello con mi padre. Mi padre empujo unos de mis hermanos pero el camion le pego y lo mato. De espues, Tomas Castillo, mi hermano mayor era el Jefe the los Castillos."

[We returned to Mexico after the American Army, this time, killed my father, Chief Trinidad. One day the men of the family were walking back from working the fields when a big Army truck struck my father. My father us able to push my brothers out of the way but he was struck and killed. After that, Tomas Castillo, my eldest brother was the Chief of the Castillos.]

"Los Castillos no, otra vez, no tenemos confianza a los Americanos. En otra situiason, a mi Tambien me paso algo mal con los Americanos, esta ves la Inmigracion. Despues de tabajando de migrante y ahorrando suficente dinero, me compre un nuevo coche in los Estatdos Unidos. Cuando llege a la frontera no me dejaron passar con me coche. Me preguntaron que como una persona como yo puede tener un coche as se. Los escuche y en engles estavan hablando que me yvan a poner in la carcel. Me escape sin me coche y me fue a crusar la fontera para Nuevo Laredo. Nunca me regrese a los Estados Unidos. Ortra ves los Castillos no les tienen confianza al los Americanos!"

"The Castillos don't trust, again, don't trust the Americans. In another situation I too had something bad happen to me with the U.S. Immigration. After working as a migrant and saving enough money I bought me a new car in the U.S. When I got to the boarder the Border Patrol didn't let me pass and pulled me to one side. They asked me how someone like me could have such a car. I overheard them talking in English that they were going to arrest me. I escaped and went to cross the border and went into Nuevo Laredo, never to return to the U.S. again. Again, the Castillo's can't trust the Americans!"

Appendix C
Common Comanche Chief Names
(Castillo, 2023)

Documented Comanche Chiefs by Name
(* Spanish Names, non-translated)

Texts Indian Papers Vol I [53a]

Muestyah
Muguara
Muhy
Pah-Hah-Yuco

Texas Indian Papers Vol II [53b]

Aka-Chua-Ta
Pochanaquarhip (Buffalo Hump)
Chom-O-Pardua
Cut Arm (English Translation)
Ta.Na.cio Quache (Bears Tail)
Ta-Sha.ro.she
Yetcpt (aka: Santa Anna)
Mopechucope
Nouishawipe
Pahaencah
Pah-hah-yuco
Powauca
Qua-Hora-Poah
Sa-Koya-Kah
Sa-Vi-Ah (Small Wolf)
Tuna-Woora-Quashi
Wabeoukeac
Wadacanapsa
Wagon Bowles (English Translation)

Texas Indian Papers Vol III [53c]

Car-A-Wa (Never Stops)
Carno-San-Tua
Ceacheneca
Chip-Es-Se-Ah
Cush-Un-A-Rah-A
*Guadalupe

Texas Indian Papers III cont'd

Qua-Ha-No
Pe-Ah-Tie-Quosh
 (Rifle Breach)
Mo-He-Ka (Pole cat)
Ho-Chu-Ca
Ish-Shu-Ku
Ish-A-Me-A-Qui
Ka-He-Na-Bo-Ne
Kai-He-Na-Nom-Ha
Kai-Tia-Ta
Ka-Nah-u-Mah-Ka
Ke-Wid-Da-Wip-Pa
Koo-Chi-Ta-Ku
Tecueshe
Ta-Bup-Ta
Sanaco
Sah-Vi-Artee
Quarah-Ha-Poo-E
Po-Hu-Ca-Wa-Kit
Pe-Ah-Tie-Quosh
Parrow-a-Kifty
Pa-Na-Che
Pah-Moo-Wa-Ta
Pah-Hah-Yoco
O-Ka-Art-Su
Oho-is
O-Ha-Wa-Kit
Mon-Ne-Con-Nah-Heh
Moo-Ra-Que-Top
Ma-War-Ra
Weit-Che-Ki
 (Hummingbird)
Lambshead
 (English Translation)

Texas Indian Papers
 III cont'd
Ka-Bah-Ha-Moo (Never Smokes)
Ka-Tumpas (also Ketumse)
Toshwa (White)

Texas Indian Papers Vol IV [53d]
Mochecut
A-Quo-Ha-da   (Black Beard)
Baja Sol (Translated to Spanish)

Texas Indian Papers Vol V [53e]
Poohevequasoo (Iron Jacket, Camisa de Fiero)
 [English and Spanish Translations]
Ka-Kar-A-Way
Katemsee
No-Co-Nee
To-Sha-Way

Uair.Library.Arizona.edu
*Pedro Ygnacio Ysampampi Sanchez
Equera Capa
Soxas
Soquina
Sojais
Cabesa Rapada (Spanish translation)
*Vizente
Rallado (Spanish translation)
Paruaranimuco

Myths and Legends of the Lipan Apache [54]
Madzit

Comanche Empire [51]
Awahakei
Barbaquista
Big Fat Fall (a tripping)
 [English Translation]
Big Tree
(English Translation)
Bigotes (Spanish Translation)
Blanco (Spanish Translation)
Canaquaipe
Chihuahua

Comanche Empire Cont'd
Cuerno Verde (Spanish Translation)
Cuetaninaveni
Drinking (English Translation)
Ecueracapa
Encanaguane'
Eschas
Guersec
Guik'a'te
Guonique

Comanche Empire Cont'd

El Cojo (Spansih Translation)
Cordero
Cota de Malla (Spanish Translation)
Is-Sa-Keep
Ishocoly
Maque
Moara
Mopechocope
Mountain of Rocks
Mowway
Muguara
Nimiricante
Onacama
El Oso (Spanish Translation)
Pacer (Spanish Translation)
Paraqinanchi
Paruacoom
Paruakevitsi
Paruanarimuca
Paruaquita
Paruasemena
Petanocona
Pinto (Spanish Translation)
Pisimampat
Pisinampe
Papaibos
Pareiya
Povea
Prick in the Forehead
 (English translation)
Quannah Parker
Queque
Quenoc
Qui-Te-Sain
Quihuaneantime

Comanche Empire Cont'd

Hachaxas
Hichapat
Satank
Satanta
Sitting Bull
 (English Translation)
Sofais
Sohuacat
Somiquaso
El Sordo (Deaf one)
 (Both Spanish and
 English Translations)
Tabequana (Sun Eagle)
Tave-Pete
Tebenanaka (Sound of the Sun)
Tichinalla
Toro Echicero (Sorcerer Bull)
 (Spanish Translation)
Toro Blanco
 (Spanish Translation)
Tosacondata
Tosapoy
Tosawa
Toyamancare
Tutsayatuhouit
 (black prairie dog)
Yellow Wolf
 (English Translation)
Yzazat

Out of the 147 name samplings, from 9 sources, only 3 were actual "Spanish names". That is, not a name Translated from Comanche to Spanish. That is 2% of all names sampled. The probability that "Castillo" was a Comanche name, much less a Comanche Chief's name, is extremely unlikely.

Also noteworthy is that all 3 of the Spanish names, (Pedro, Vicente, and Guadalupe) were Biblical Names. Whereas "Castillo" is not a Biblical name.

Appendix D

Common Lipan and Comanche finger pointing and other accusations
(Castillo, 2023)
(Blaming each other)

The Lipan Apache and the Comanche had a long history of blaming each other to the U.S. Government, Texas Government, and the Spanish Government. This was done to relinquish themselves of wrong doings as well as to take credit for "good" things. There many instances of this finger pointing here are but a few....

1771 : (Robinson 2013) "I Fought a Good Fight" pgs 100, 104

4/1774 : (Uair.library.arizona.edu/item/214003)

10/1785 : (Uair.library.arizona.edu/item/226332)

1790 : (Robinson 2013) "I Fought a Good Fight" pg 151

1/1845 : (Winfrey/Day 1995) "Texas Indian Papers Vol II" pg 168

7/1845 : (Winfrey/Day 1995) "Texas Indian Papers Vol II" pg 293

3/1854 : (Minor 2009) "Turning Adversity into Advantage pg 165

Summer/1854 : (Minor 2009) "Turning Adversity into Advantage pg 171

(Texas Dept. of Transportation 2021) Tribal Histories Comanche Nation Research Report pg 39-40
[https://ftp.txdot.gov/pub/txdot-info/env/toolkit/415-03-rpt.pdf]

Appendix E

Origin of Castillo as Lipan Name

(Castillo, 2023)

Chief Roque has been noted in several documents.

Britten, Thomas A (2009) "The Lipan Apaches: People of Wind and Lighting" pg.143

McGown-Minor, Nancy (2009) "Turning Adversity to Advantage: A History of the Lipan

 Apaches of Texas and Northern Mexico, 1700-1900" pgs. 98, 112, 123

1779 Cabello to Cavaier de Croix, Sept. 3, Reel 11 Vol. 87, Bexar Archives

1787 Curvelo to Rafael Martinez Pacheco, Sept. 15, Reel 17, Vol. 146, Baxer Archives

1791 Munoz to Pedro de Nava, Jan. 24, AGM, PI 2Q215, Vol. 530 The Center for

 American History

Lipan Chief Roque served as primary Chief from 1779-1791 [53]

It is important to recognize that Nancy McGown-Minor, through her research for her books "Turning Adversity to Advantage" (2009) pg. 98, Then again in "The Light Gray People" pg. 106, noted that "Castle" was an alias for Chief Roque. "Castle", in English, is "Castillo" translated to Spanish.

Also important is that the Spanish language most likely would have been used as opposed to the English language at the time, so the alias suggested would have been for "Castillo" and not "Castle", which may have been used in those works since they targeted English readers. This could have come about since Roque and Castillo can be used interchangeably in Spanish, French and the Portuguese Language in certain situations, for instance in the strategical game of chess.

The name likely morphed from (Lipan): tse' [rock] -------
Roque (Spanish translation of tse'),
{or Castillo} ----- (Spanish alias): Castillo

Appendix F

Message from President of United States to the 2nd session of the 33rd Congress

Congress

(Reports of General P.F. Smith Commander of Army Headquarters in Texas)

33D CONGRESS, }   SENATE.   { Ex. Doc.
2d Session. }   { No. 1.

MESSAGE

FROM THE

PRESIDENT OF THE UNITED STATES

TO THE

TWO HOUSES OF CONGRESS,

AT THE

COMMENCEMENT OF THE SECOND SESSION

OF

THE THIRTY-THIRD CONGRESS.

DECEMBER 4, 1854.—Read, and ordered to be printed with the accompanying documents, and that 10,000 extra copies be printed for the use of the Senate.

PART II.

WASHINGTON :
BEVERLEY TUCKER, SENATE PRINTER.
1854.

28   REPORT OF THE

REPORTS FROM THE DEPARTMENT OF TEXAS.

HEADQUARTERS DEPARTMENT OF TEXAS,
Corpus Christi, May 10, 1854.

COLONEL: I have the honor to transmit, herewith, a report from Assistant Surgeon E. W. Johns, of an attack on a train twelve miles beyond Fort Ewell, and of the pursuit he caused to be made of the aggressors. I beg leave to call the notice of the general to the prompt, efficient, and skilful measures taken by Assistant Surgeon Johns on this occasion.

It must be observed that as there was reason to expect some expedition on the part of the Indians, several small parties having been seen last moon, all the men that could be spared from the posts were out on scouts, and at Fort Ewell every officer was in the field except Lieutenant Howland, who was sick in bed, leaving the command of the post for some time in the hands of Dr. Johns, assistant surgeon there. Assistant Surgeon Head had just arrived and relieved Dr. Johns; but being a stranger to the country, had left the arrangement of the pursuit to the latter. The non-commissioned officers in charge of the parties sent out, and the men, I know to be as good as any in the army; and of their ability and disposition to render a good account of the enemy, if they can overtake him, I have no doubt; but it is hardly fifty miles to the Rio Grande, and the country is mostly thick chaparral, and hard and dry, retaining little impression of a trail.

I think the party was Lipans and Seminoles, and had just crossed from Mexico. Among the detachments out was one of two non-commisioned officers and eighteen men, from Fort Merrill, under Lieutenant G. Cosby. On Monday he was at Lake Trinidad, about forty miles from this towards Laredo, with half of his command, where he attacked and routed a party of more than forty Indians, killing three and wounding several, and taking all their plunder.

I am sorry to record the loss of Sergeant Byrne, a gallant and good soldier, who fell fighting, pierced with many arrows. Several of the men were wounded, and two are missing. I am afraid they were killed in the chaparral.

Lieutenant Cosby was severely, but not dangerously, wounded in the sword-arm, and his clothes are pierced by arrows. He met Lieutenant Roger Jones shortly after the Indians retreated, who continued the pursuit with sixteen men.

I have no terms to speak my sense of the gallantry and coolness displayed by Lieutenant Cosby in this affair. I beg to call it particularly to the notice of the General, and to beg that some way may be devised for affording to the men the reward they merit for their good conduct, which in this case was conspicuous, having been deserted in the outset by sixteen well mounted and armed rancheros.

Lieutenant Cosby was brought in this moning in a wagon, to receive

117

surgical assistance, there not being a medical officer in the department to accompany any detachment to the field.

Ascertaining, by the occurrences recited, that the Indians are in some force below the line of posts, I have already despatched the order, a copy of which is enclosed, and will leave no steps untaken to destroy the aggressors.

There are 300 recruits wanted to fill up the rifle regiment, and they could now occupy the posts, and leave all the old soldiers for the field.

 • • • • • •

With the highest respect, your obedient servant,

PERSIFOR F. SMITH,
Bvt. Maj. Gen. Com'g Dept.

Lieut. Col. LORENZO THOMAS,
 Assistant Adjutant General, Headquarters of the Army.

P. S.—Lieutenant Cosby says the guides pronounce the Indians he attacked to be Lipans, and their chief they recognise as a man of consequence, named Castillo.

P. F. S.

———

HEADQUARTERS DEPARTMENT OF TEXAS,
Corpus Christi, May 15, 1854.

COLONEL: In my report of the 10th instant, transmitting Assistant Surgeon E. W. Johns's account of an attack on a train near Fort Ewell, I said: " The non-commissioned officers in charge of the parties sent out, and the men, I know to be as good as any in the army; and of their ability and disposition to render a good account of the enemy, if they can overtake him, I have no doubt."

I have now the honor to transmit a report from Assistant Surgeon J. Frazier Head, commanding officer at Fort Ewell, announcing the return of the parties, and I hope the General will see in the result of their pursuit a full justification of the confidence I placed in the parties.

It must be observed that the three detachments, each under the first sergeant of its company, joined together, and, without a guide, pressed the pursuit across a country of the most unfavorable kind for eighty miles without a drop of water for either man or horse, and then continued it twenty-five miles further, until they overtook the Indians. These escaped with their persons, as they can always do near a thick chaparral, but lost their plunder, baggage, animals, trophies, and some of their own arms.

I beg to lay before the General, in terms of the highest commendation, the names of First Sergeant C. H. McNally, company D, regiment mounted rifles, who commanded the detachments united; First Sergeant John Green, company B, same regiment; and First Sergeant John Williams, company G, same regiment. I also enclose the post order issued by Dr. Head, and express my concurrence in his praise of the whole command.

I have understood from Colonel Neighbors, Indian agent, and from a report brought to Ringgold barracks, that three or four hundred Indians are assembled at the place occupied by the Seminoles, under

" Wild Cat," in Coahuila, Mexico, who are preparing for an inroad into Texas. It will take many more mounted men than we have to cover the frontier even up to the mouth of the Pecos. But I shall so dispose of the whole command that I hope to be able to keep them from the settlements; but I must leave the road to El Paso somewhat exposed, for there is not cavalry enough to cover it. I wish most earnestly that an additional regiment of mounted riflemen had been authorized by Congress in time for this necessity, and with the increased pay they could be easily raised.

   With high respect, your obedient servant,

         PERSIFOR F. SMITH,
       Brevet Major General Commanding Department.

Lieut. Col. L. Thomas,
 Assistant Adjutant General, Headquarters of the Army.

    HEADQUARTERS DEPARTMENT OF TEXAS,
       Corpus Christi, July 15, 1854.

COLONEL: Preparatory to moving the regiment of mounted riflemen from the Nueces to the Rio Grande, in conformity with the instructions of the War Department, the companies were ordered to be got ready, and Brevet Lieutenant Colonel Roberts, commanding Fort Ewell, called in all the detachments from that post; thus uncovering the Rio Grande from Laredo down. Lieutenant Colonel Seawell, at Ringgold barracks, and Colonel Loomis, at Fort McIntosh, immediately reported that small parties of Indians were crossing the river at various places, and committing robberies and murders. I immediately ordered some companies to the river again, and directed the detachment from Fort Merrill, that had been withdrawn from Santa Gertrude's (forty miles from this) on account of the men having the scurvy, to be replaced there; but at 3 o'clock a. m., on the 14th, an express from up the road informed me that Indians had killed some persons at " Proscenius," twenty-five miles north of Santa Gertrudes. I then ordered another detachment from Fort Merrill towards the former place.

In the mean time, on the 4th of July, Captain Van Buren, of the rifles, with eleven men and two non-commissioned officers, was sent by the commander of Fort Inge to scout in the direction of the Rio Grande. Near Lake Espantosa he met a party of 8th infantry from Fort Clarke mounted on mules; they had followed the trail of Indians who had come from the northward, and their animals were broken down. Captain Van Buren took up the trail, and followed it to the southward with unsurpassed diligence and under great difficulties until, on the 11th, in the evening, he met them about thirteen miles from " Proscenius," towards the southwest; they were thirty, and he had thirteen men in all. He attacked them boldly, and the Indians at first stood their ground. Their chief, however, was killed, and his body remained in Captain Van Buren's possession; four other Indians fell, but were picked up by their companions. Captain Van Buren was badly wounded in the arm, but dismounted his men to use their rifles more effectually. He soon routed the Indians, who fled, leaving some horses, many lances and shields, and other trophies; but I regret to say that Captain Van Buren himself was shot through the body with an arrow, entering just above the sword-belt, and coming out *through* it behind. His wound is very dangerous. He had two men wounded, and his horse was shot in the head. In this situation he could not pursue, but sent a corporal and two men to Fort Ewell for a surgeon and ambulance. As these did not arrive, next day he despatched two other men to meet and bring them in; but these got lost, and, finding a trail, followed it until they reached Palo Alto, twenty-five miles from here. From this place they came here, and I immediately despatched Second Lieutenant Roger Jones, with nine riflemen that were waiting as escort for my departure for El Paso. Dr. McParlin, who was here also to accompany me, went with them with an ambulance.

The party, however, that went to Fort Ewell returned with twenty men, under Lieutenant Colonel Roberts, and were bringing Captain Van Buren here when they met Lieutenant Jones at Palo Alto. Col. Roberts was attacked with the dysentery on the march, and returned to Fort Ewell with his command.

The guide of Captain Van Buren, who is a Lipan Indian, says these Indians are Comanches, and the one killed a chief of consequence.

It is reported that another party of Indians is down, twenty-five in number.

Captain Van Buren has just come in, but the surgeon desires that he may be kept quiet.

I respectfully recommend his conduct in a pursuit of over two hundred miles, and in the action, to the consideration of the government. As the mail goes immediately, I will defer sending his report till next mail.

With the highest respect, your obedient servant,
PERSIFOR F. SMITH,
Brevet Major General.

Lieut. Col. L. Thomas,
Assistant Adjutant General, Headquarters of the Army.

The surgeon says of Captain Van Buren's wound that it is very dangerous, and it will be extraordinary if he recovers.

P. F. S.

[Extract.]

HEADQUARTERS DEPARTMENT OF TEXAS,
"Painted Camp," on the Limpia, Oct. 9, 1854.

COLONEL: I have the honor to transmit a report from Captain J. G. Walker, of the rifles, of a pursuit of a party of Indians, and an action with them and their tribe on the 3d inst. Captain Walker was in command of my escort. We left El Paso on the 28th of September, and at 2 p. m. on the 1st instant arrived at Eagle spring, having marched, in the four days, 121 miles, and on the last day 35. We met, about 14 miles from the Rio Grande, a party driving cattle, who reported that on the morning of the preceding day, at Eagle spring,

Appendix G

Lipan Apache Documented Locations in the spring and summer of 1854

Accounts that put Lipan in the close vicinity (within 200 mi) at the time of Chief Castillo's last days:

1. Nueces River Headwaters (March 1854) [35]
2. At Fort Inge, Uvalde, Texas (March 1854) [36]
3. On Nueces River (April 1854) [37]
4. In Laredo, Texas (April 1854) [38]
5. On Nueces River, Near Corpus Christi, Texas (May 1854) [39]
6. Most Lipan near Ft Inge, Uvalde, Texas (May 1854) [40]
7. On Nueces River (July 1854) [41]
8. At Ft. Inge, Uvalde, Texas (July 1854) [42]
9. Chief Castillo's main encampment at/near Agua Dulce, Texas (July, 1854) [54]
10. "Chief Castillo" was killed on July 11, 1854. After his group was attacked by the U.S. Army near Ben Bolt, Texas at Trinidad Lake (about 10 miles from San Diego, Texas as a crow flies) or about 45 miles from Fort Merrill at Dinero, Texas. [28a-28g] (map 3)

To further add, and to note, is that during that time (March – July 1854) according to reports the **Southern Comanche** were:

1. At Clear Fork of the Brazos (425 mi away) (March 1854) [43]
2. At San Saba (300 mi away) (April 1854) [44]
3. In Chihuahua, Mexico (April 1854) [45]

Northern Comanche were living between the Red River and the Colorado River (1854) [46]

Appendix H

Lipan "Roque's" and "Castillo's" mentioned in publications.

- ### Chief Roque (1779)
1779 Cabello to Cavalier de Croix, Oct 19, Reel11, Vol. 88 Baxer Archives

- ### Chief Roque (1787)
1787 Curvelo to Rafael Martinez Pacheco, Sept. 15, Reel 17, Vol. 146, Baxer Archives

- ### Son of Chief Roque (1791)
[possible grandfather of Chief Castillo]
1791 Munoz to Pedro de Nava, Jan. 24, AGM, *PI,* 2Q186, Vol.530, The Center for American History

- ### Headman Castillo (1844)
Winfrey/Day (1966) "The Indian Papers of Texas and the Southwest, 1825-1916"
Vol II :97

- ### Chief Castillo: (1844)
Minor (2009) "Turning Adversity into Advantage" :146

- ### Chief Castillo: (1854)
Robinson (2013) "I Fought a Good Fight" :242

- ## Chief Castillo (1854)

  http://www.cclibraries.com/localhistory/oldbayview/index.php/lit-of-burials/696-michael-e-van-burenx

- ## Chief Castillo (1854)

  Message from the **President of the United States** to Congress. May 10, 1854

  https://play.google.com/books/reader?id=OQ1FAQAAMAAJ&printsec=frontcover&output=reader&hl=en&pg=GBS.PA29

Part II - My Ancestral Journey
Works Cited

Citations:

1) Birth Certificate – Thomas R Castillo; Texas Department of State Health Services
2) WWII Draft Card – Reyes S. Castillo; National Archives and Records Administration (NARA)
3) 1930 U.S. Federal Census Precinct 3 Gonzales, Texas, USA. ref. Tomas Castillo, Reyes Castillo; NARA, Roll: 2337; Page: 13B; Enumeration District 10; Image: 311.0
4) Death Certificate – Trinidad Castillo ref: Pablo Castillo, Tomas Castillo; Texas Department of State Health Services
5) Death Certificate – Tomas Castillo ref: Reyes S Castillo, Trinidad Castillo; Texas Department of State Health Services
6) Marriage Registration – Trinidad Castillo & Mariana Quinones, Dr Arroyo N.L. ref: Indigenous Person, Pablo Castillo; Nuevo Leon, Mexico, Civil Registration Marriages 1859-1960; ancestry.com, 2015
7) Oral History - Emilio Castillo, 2006; Nuevo Laredo, Nuevo Leon, Mex. Deposition by Thomas R Castillo (2023), Appendix A
8) Lipan Vs. U.S., Mexico, Texas Rangers, Texas Settlers, Other Tribes and Diseases:
   a. Ray/Opler (1974) "Apache Indians Vol X": 365
   b. Wikipedia: "Department of New Mexico"; https://en.wikipedia.org/w/index.php?title=Department_of_New_Mexico&oldid=1145042237
   c. Smith (1964) "The Scalp Hunters in the Borderlands 1835-1850" Arizona and the West Vol 6 No. 1 Spring 1964; Journal of the Southwest:
   d. Winfrey/Day (1995) Texas State Historical Association: "The Indian Papers of Texas and the Southwest 1825-1915 Vol V":162
   e. Minor (2009) "Turning Adversity to Advantage" (A history of the Lipan Apaches of TX and Northern Mexico 1700-1900): 156, 173
   f. Britten (2009) "The Lipan Apache" (People of Wind and Lighting): 216-219
9) Marriage Registration - Pablo Castillo & Isidra Lira El Venado, SLP, Mexico ref: Indigenous person, Anastacio Castillo; Direccion Estatal del Registro Civil del Estado de San Luis Potosi, Mexico; San Luis Potosi, Mexico, Civil Registrations Marriages, 1860-

1967; Ancestry.com 2015

10) Birth of Longinos Castillo – March 24, 1872; Venado, SLP, Mexico; ref: Pablo Castillo, Anastacio Castillo; Direccion Estatal del Registro Civil del Estado de San Luis Potosi; San Luis Potosi, Mexico, Civil Registration Births, 1860-1947; Ancestry.com 2015

11) Lipan "Castillo's" documented in publications.
   a. Robinson (2013) "I Fought a Good Fight": 242
   b. Minor (2009) "Turning Adversity into Advantage": 146
   c. https://obc.cclibraries.com/list/tv/van-buren-michael-e
   d. Winfrey/Day (1966) "The Indian Papers of Texas and the Southwest, 1825-1916" Vol II : 97
   e. Message from the President of the United States to Congress, May 10, 1854 https://play.google.com/books/reader?id=OQ1FAQAAMAAJ&printsec=frontcover&output=reader&hl=en&pg=GBS.PA29
   f. Oral History - Emilio Castillo, 2006; Nuevo Laredo, Nuevo Leon, Mex. Deposition by Thomas R Castillo (2023), Appendix A

12) La Apacheria en el siglo XIX (2):1 https://apacheria.es/apacheria-siglo-xlx-2/

13) Death Registration – Pablo Castillo Matehuala, SLP, Mexico; April 29, 1925; ref: Parents Unknown; San Luis Potosi, Mexico, Civil Registration Deaths, 1860-1987; Ancestry.com 2015

14) Buchenau (2015) "The Mexican Revolution, 1910-1946": 10 https://doi.org/10.1093/acrefore/9780199366439.013.21

15) Boarder Crossing Card issued by U.S. Dept of Labor – Trinidad Castillo; January 23, 1928 Laredo, TX USA ; The National Archives and Records Administration, Washington D.C. ; Nonstatistical Manifests and Statistical Index Cards of Aliens Arriving at Laredo, TX May 1903 – November 1929; NAI 2843448; Record Group Title: Records of the Immigration and Naturalization Service, 1787-2004.; Record group Number: 85; Microfilm Roll Number: 013; Ancestry.com 2006

16) Obituary – Reyes S,Castillo died October 10, 2019 https://www.dignitymemorial.com/obituaries/corpus-christi-tx/reyes-castillo-8886194

17) Obituary – Rosa C. Caballero died January 1, 2021 https://www.dignitymemorial.com/obituaries/corpus-christi-tx/rosa-caballero-9979356

18) U.S. Army record/report - Trinidad Castillo killed by U.S. Army Truck – Not yet available. Unknown classification.

19) Enciso (2017) – "They Should Stay There": (The story of Mexican Migration and Repatriation during the Great Depression); ISBN: 9781469634265

20) Death of Amilio (Emilio) Q Castillo; Nuevo Laredo, Tamaulipas,MX

21) 1860 New Mexico Census; ref: Jose Pablo Castillo – Indian, Anastacio Castillo – Head of Household; The National Archives in Washington D.C.: Record Group: Records of the Bureau of the Census; Record group Number:29; Series Number:M653; Residence Date: 1860; Home in 1860: Valencia, Valencia, New Mexico Territory; Roll: M653_716; Page: 6; Family History Library Film:803716; Ancestry.com 2009

22) Marriage Registration Tomas Castillo and Petra Rodriguez; Nuevo Laredo, Tamaulipas, MX; "Mexico Tamaulipas, Registro Civil 1800-2002"; FamilySearch https://www.familysearch.org/ark:/61903/1:1:QGMR-9NQR : Sat Oct 28 04:20:29 UTC 2023

23   a) Redd (2018) "Governments Used to Pay For Native American Scalps Which Made Scalping a Booming Business"; HISTORY COLLECTION https://historycollection.com/governments-used-to-pay-for-native-american-scalps-which-made-scalping-a-booming-business/

23   b) Smith (1964): "The Scalp Hunter in the Borderlands 1835-1850" ;Arizona and the West, Vol 6, No. 1 (Spring, 1964). Pgs 5-22, Journal of the Southwest; http://www.jstor.org/stable/40167089

24)   a) Adams (1991) "Embattled Borderland: Northern Nuevo Leon and the Indios Barbaros, 1686-1870" pg.211
        b) Anderson (2005) "The Conquest of Texas" pg.254
        c) Britten (2009) "The Lipan Apache" (People of Wind and Lighting) pg. 217
        d) La Vere (2004) "The Oldest Apache" pg. 196-197
        e) Minor (2009b) "Turning Adversity to Advantage "(A history of the Lipan Apache of TX and Northern Mexico 1700-1900) pg.154
        f) Ray/Opler (1974) "Apache Indians Vol X" pg.131
        g) Robinson (2013) Robinson (2013) "I Fought a Good Fight: A History of the Lipan Apaches" pgs. 243, 248
        h) Winfrey/Day (1995) "The Indian Papers of Texas and the Southwest 1825-1915: Vol V, pg. 162

25) Minor (2009a) "The Light Gray People: An Ethno-History of the Lipan Apaches of Texas and Northern Mexico" pg93

26   a) Tonkawa tribe of Oklahoma List of Principle Chiefs https://www.worldstatesmen.org/US_NativeAM.html
        b) Chief Broken Eagle [Hernandez](2022) "The Path I Follow"; The More Things Change; The Menard News: https://www.menardnews.com/news/more-things-change-4

    c) The Nation: Apr. 11, 1867; "WHY DO THE TONKAWAH EAT THE COMANCHES?"; Correspondence: To the Editor of the Nation; W.A.

27   a) Captain Michael E. Van Buren; Old Bayview Cemetery (printed Pg 1) https://obc.cclibraries.com/list/tv/van-buren-michael-e

    b) Captain Michael E. Van Buren; Old Bayview Cemetery (printed Pg 2) https://obc.cclibraries.com/list/tv/van-buren-michael-e

    c) Captain Michael E. Van Buren; Old Bayview Cemetery (printed Pg 3) https://obc.cclibraries.com/list/tv/van-buren-michael-e

    d) Captain Michael E. Van Buren; Old Bayview Cemetery (printed Pg 5) https://obc.cclibraries.com/list/tv/van-buren-michael-e

    e) Captain Michael E. Van Buren; Old Bayview Cemetery (printed Pg 7) https://obc.cclibraries.com/list/tv/van-buren-michael-e

    f) Captain Michael E. Van Buren; Old Bayview Cemetery (printed Pg 8) https://obc.cclibraries.com/list/tv/van-buren-michael-e

    g) Captain Michael E. Van Buren; Old Bayview Cemetery (printed Pg 9) https://obc.cclibraries.com/list/tv/van-buren-michael-e

28) Castillo (2023b) "Recorded Comanche Chiefs Name - Sample Compilation". Appendix B

29) Message from the President of the United States to the Two Houses of Congress; 33D Congress, 2nd Session; Ex Doc No. 1; December 4, 1854 Report from Secretary of War of Headquarters Department of Texas Corpus Christi. https://play.google.com/books/reader?id=OQ1FAQAAMAAJ&pg=GBS.PA28&printsec=frontcover&output=reader&hl=en&pg=GBS.PA29

30) Castillo (2023) "Common Lipan and Comanche Finger Pointing" (Blaming each other) Compilation of Sources Appendix C

31) Castillo (2025) "Lipan Chief Castillo - 1854"

32) Smith (1963) "Indians in American-Mexican Relations Before the War of 1846"; Hispanic American Historical Review (1963) 43(1):34-64 https://doi.org/10.1215/00182168-43.1.34

33) Winfrey/Day (1995) Vol V pg. 161 https://www.nps.gov/parkhistory/online_books/amis/aspr-34/app4_files/sheet008.htm

34) Winfrey/Day (1995) Vol V pg. 161 https://www.nps.gov/parkhistory/online_books/amis/aspr-34/app4_files/sheet008.htm

35) Winfrey/Day (1995) Vol V pg. 183 https://www.nps.gov/ parkhistory/online_books/amis/aspr-34/app4_files/sheet008.htm

36) Winfrey/Day (1995) Vol V pg. 170 https://www.nps.gov/ parkhistory/online_books/amis/aspr-34/app4_files/sheet008.htm

37) BIA 2: 680 https://www.nps.gov/parkhistory/online_books/amis/ aspr-34/app4_files/sheet008.htm

38) BIA 2: 793 https://www.nps.gov/parkhistory/online_books/amis/ aspr-34/app4_files/sheet008.htm

39) BIA 2: 640 https://www.nps.gov/parkhistory/online_books/amis/ aspr-34/app4_files/sheet008.htm

40) BIA 2: 647 https://www.nps.gov/parkhistory/online_books/amis/ aspr-34/app4_files/sheet008.htm

41) BIA 2: 384 https://www.nps.gov/parkhistory/online_books/amis/ aspr-34/app4_files/sheet008.htm

42) BIA 1: 755 https://www.nps.gov/parkhistory/online_books/amis/ aspr-34/app4_files/sheet008.htm

43) BIA 2: 762 https://www.nps.gov/parkhistory/online_books/amis/ aspr-34/app4_files/sheet008.htm

44) BIA 2: 762 https://www.nps.gov/parkhistory/online_books/amis/ aspr-34/app4_files/sheet008.htm

45) Winfrey/Day (1995) "The Indian Papers of Texas and the Southwest 1825-1915" Vol V   pg. 170 https://www.nps.gov/ parkhistory/online_books/amis/aspr34/app4_files/sheet008.htm

46) Wallace (1987) "The Comanches, Lords of the South Plains" pg. 310 https://www.nps.gov/parkhistory/online_books/amis/ aspr-34/app4_files/sheet008.htm

47) Menchaca (2002): 109 "Recovering History, Constructing Race: The Indian, Black and White Roots of Mexican Americans"

48) Papers relating to the foreign relations of the United States / transmitted to Congress with the annual message of the President. (1965) call # Z1236.L45 21707-79 United States Dept. of State https://portal.tamucc.edu/search/?seartchtype= 0&searcharg=19135414

49) Pekka Hamalainen (2008): "Comanche Empire"

50) Schilz (1987): Lipan Apaches in Texas

51)   a) Winfrey/Day (1995) "The Indian Papers of Texas and the Southwest 1825-1915" Vol. I

        b) Winfrey/Day (1995) "The Indian Papers of Texas and the Southwest 1825-1915" Vol. II

        c) Winfrey/Day (1995) "The Indian Papers of Texas and the Southwest 1825-1915" Vol. III

        d) Winfrey/Day (1995) "The Indian Papers of Texas and the Southwest 1825-1915" Vol.IV

        e) Winfrey/Day (1995) "The Indian Papers of Texas and the Southwest 1825-1915" Vol. V

52) Opler (1940) "Myths and Legends of the Lipan Apache Indians"
53) Minor (2009) "The Light Gray People: An Ethno-History of the Lipan Apaches of Texas and Northern Mexico: pg. 106
54) Wooster, R. (1995) "Recollections of Western Texas 1852-55 : By Two of the Mounted Rifles" pg. 86

Maps

Pictures and Illustrations

Pictures:

1) "American Bison In Texas"; Courtesy of Lucille Contreras and the Texas Tribal Buffalo Project. **Pg.13**

2a) "Buckskin Clothing"; Source: Berlanier (1969) "The Indians of Texas in 1830" (Open Domain) Credit: Watercolor by - Lino Sanchez y Tapia after Jose Maria Sanchez Y Tapia **Pg.14**

2b) "Lipan Cotton Clothing"; Source Credit: Courtesy of Anabeth and Ruben Cordova   (2012 McAllen, Texas) **Pg.14**

3) "South Texas Chaparral"; Courtesy of the Red Sun Ranch (Juan and Melinda Villarreal) **Pg.13**

4) "Lipan Warrior"; Source: Open Domain, Credit: According to Dessin de Gilbert, Photo by J. Laurent (1842 – Mexico) **Pg.47**

5) "Peyote – The Medicine" Courtesy: Andres Gutierrez Camarillo **Pg.51**

Illustrations:

Front Cover Top - *"South Texas Lipan Warrior"*

Credit: Noe Bazan (2025) Lipan Apache

Front Cover Bottom - *"Nopal Family Tree"*

Credit: Coral Castillo (2025) Lipan Apache

Bibliography

Adams (1991) "Embattled Borderland: Northern Nuevo Leon and the Indios Barbaros, 1686-1870"

Alsonzo, Alexander (2022) "Until It's Too Late: The Battle of Fort Buchanan"

Alonzo (2015) "La Apacheria en el siglo XIX (2)"

Anderson, Gary C. (2005) "The Conquest of Texas: Ethnic Cleansing in the Promised Land"

Berlandier, Jean Louis (1969) "Indians of Texas in 1830"

Bigelow, Michael E; Command Historian (July-September 2012) "A Short History of Army Intelligence" U.S. Army Intelligence and Security Command

Britten, Thomas (2009) "The Lipan Apache: People of Wind and Lighting"

Brown Jr., Tom (1993) "Grandfather: A Native American's lifelong search for truth and harmony with nature"

Buchenau (2015) "The Mexican Revolution, 1910-1946"

Bucklew (2010) "Life of F.M. Bucklew (The Indian Captive)"

Castillo (2023) "Commonality of Lipan and Comanche Finger Pointing"

Castillo (2023) "Lipan Apache Chief Castillo's Last Days"

Castillo, Emilio (2006) Interview conducted by T. Castillo "Castillo Family Clan Oral History of Emilio Castillo"

Castillo (2023) "Recorded Comanche Chief's Sampling of Names – Compilation"

Chief Broken Eagle [Hernandez] (2022) "The Path I Follow"

Day/Jones/Kelly/Myers/Nunn/Richardson/Simpson/Winfrey (1971) "Indian Tribes of Texas (Alabama-Coushatta, Caddo, Comanche, Karankawa, Kiowa, Lipan Apache, Tonkawa, Wichita)"

de la Garza (2013) "From the REPUBLIC of the RIO GRANDE"

Delay (2008) "War of a Thousand Deserts (Indian Raids and the U.S. – Mexican War)"

DeShields (1993) "Border Wars of Texas"

Edge, Laura B (2016) "The Lipan Apache"

Enciso (2017) "They Should Stay There"

Flores, Dan (1991) *The Journal of American History*

EX Doc No. 1 (1854) "Message from the President of the United States to the Two Houses of Congress: 33D Congress, 2nd Session"

Givens, Murphy (2016) *Corpus Christi Caller-Times*

Gorenfeld, Will (2018) :The Battle of Cieneguilla: Dragoons vs. Jicarilla Apaches"

Grimm (1952,1994) "Collins, TX (Nueces County)"

Grimm (1976,2020) "Los Presenos, TX"

Habig, Marion A. (1968) "The Alamo Chain of Missions: A History of San Antonio's Five Old Missions"

Ingslad/Stenehjem (2004) "The Apache Indians (In Search of the Missing Tribe)"

Johnson, Michael G. (2013) "American Indian Tribes of the Southwest (Men-at-Arms)"

Kaule (2018) "The Oldest Apache"

La Vere (2004) "The Texas Indians"

Laumbach, Karl W. (2002) "An Apache Battlefield of the Victorio's War"

Loughery, Robert W. (1854) *The Texas Republican* Vol.5, No.37, Ed 1 Saturday, April 8

Loughery, Robert W. (1854) *The Texas Republican* Vol.5, No. 46, Ed 1 Saturday, June 10

Menchaca (2002): "Recovering History, Constructing Race: The Indian, Black and White Roots of Mexican Americans"

Michno, Gregory F. and Michno, Susan J. (2008) "Forgotten Fights: Little-Known Raids and Skirmishes on the Frontier, 1823 to 1890"

McGown-Minor, Nancy (2009a) "The Light Gray People: An Ethno-History of the Lipan Apaches of Texas and Northern Mexico"

McGown-Minor, Nancy (2009b) "Turning Adversity to Advantage: A history of the Lipan Apache of TX and Northern Mexico 1700-1900"

Moore (2021) "Los Presenos"

Moorhead, Max L. (1968) "The Apache Frontier: Jacobo Ugarte and Spanish-Indian Relations in Northern New Spain, 1769-1791"

Morgan, Phillis (2004) *Wagon Tracks*

National Archives and Records Administration of the United States National Park Service

Newcomb Jr., W.W. (1961) "The Indians of Texas: From Prehistoric to Modern Times"

Oldham, W.S. & Marshall, John (1854) Texas State Gazette Vol. 5, no. 52, Ed. 1 Saturday, August 19

Opler, Morris E. (1940) "Myths and Legends of the Lipan Apache Indians"

Opler (1969) "Apache Odyssey" (A journey Between Two Worlds)

Opler (2009) "The Use of Peyote by the Carrizo and Lipan Apache Tribes"

Ortiz/Sturtevant (1979) "Handbook of North American Indians"

Pekka Hamalainen (2008): "Comanche Empire"

Parke, Aubrey G. (2020) *Sociology and Anthropology Honors Theses*

Perez, Gary (2024) – Interview Conducted by T. Castillo "Peyote and the Indigenous Peoples of South Texas and Northern Mexico"

Ray, Verne F & Opler, Morris E. (1974) "Apache Indians Vol X: Ethnohistorical Analysis of Documents Relating to the Apache Indians of Texas / Lipan and Mescalero Apache in Texas:"

Redd (2018) "Governments Used to Pay for Native American Scalps which made scalping a booming Business"

Registro Civil de Estado de Nuevo Leon, MX

Registro Civil de Estado de San Luis Potosi, MX

Registro Civil de Estado de Tampaulipas, MX

"Reports of Explorations and Surveys, to Ascertain the Most Practicable and Economical Route for a Railroad from the Mississippi River to the Pacific Ocean." These reports were compiled under the direction of the U.S. Secretary of War in 1853-54, as mandated by Congress, and were published in Washington in 1855-60 (University of Michigan Press) Unknown Volume...

Robinson (2003) "Apache Voices (Their Stories of Survival as Told to Eve Ball)"

Robinson Sherry (2013) "I Fought a Good Fight: A History of the Lipan Apaches"

Ruiz (1972) "Report on the Indian Tribes of Texas in 1828"

Schaefer, Stacy B. (2015) "Amada's blessings from the Peyote gardens of South Texas"

Schilz, Thomas F. (1987) "Lipan Apaches in Texas"

Schroeder, Eric (2025) Interview conducted by T. Castillo "Chief Castillo's Missing Body"

Smallwood, James M. (2004) "The Indian Texans"

Smith (1963) "Indians in American-Mexican Relations Before the War of 1846"

Smith (1964) "The Scalp Hunters in the Borderlands 1835-1850"

Smith (2008) "From Dominance to Disappearance (The Indians of Texas and the Near Southwest, 1786-1859)

Smithsonian Institution Bureau of American Ethnology (1907) "Handbook of American Indians North of Mexico" Part 1 & 2 Texas Department of State Health Services

THE NATION (1867) "Why Do The Tonkawa Eat the Comanche?"

Travis, Michael (unknown) "Arroyo Baluarte" accessed 03/15/2025

Tucker (2011) "The Encyclopedia of NORTH AMERICAN INDIAN WARS, 1607-1890, (A Political, Social, and Military History)" Vol. I

Tucker (2011) "The Encyclopedia of NORTH AMERICAN INDIAN WARS, 1607-1890, (A Political, Social, and Military History)" Vol. II

Tucker (2011) "The Encyclopedia of NORTH AMERICAN INDIAN WARS, 1607-1890, (A Political, Social, and Military History)" Vol. III

United States Dept. of the State

Utley, Robert M. (2008) "Victorio's War"

Wagner, Frank (2021) "Biography by Frank Wagner" *City of Corpus Christi Public Libraries*

Wallace (1987) "The Comanches, Lords of the South Plains"

Weber (1982) "THE MEXICAN FRONTIER 1821-1846: The American Southwest Under Mexico"

Weber (2005) "Barbaros: Spaniards and Their Savages in the Age of Enlightment"

Williams, Chad (2010) The Encyclopedia of Oklahoma History and Culture

Wikipedia (2009) "Battle of Diablo Mountains" Last modified January 22, 2025

Winfrey, Dorman H. & Day, James (1995) "The Indian Papers of Texas and the Southwest 1825-1915 Vol. I

Winfrey, Dorman H. & Day, James (1995) "The Indian Papers of Texas and the Southwest 1825-1915 Vol. II

Winfrey, Dorman H. & Day, James (1995) "The Indian Papers of Texas and the Southwest 1825-1915 Vol. III

Winfrey, Dorman H. & Day, James (1995) "The Indian Papers of Texas and the Southwest 1825-1915 Vol. IV

Winfrey, Dorman H. & Day, James (1995) "The Indian Papers of Texas and the Southwest 1825-1915 Vol. V

Wooster, Robert (1995) "Recollections of Western Texas: 1852-1855"

Websites Utilized

https://www.ancestry.com

https://apacheria.es/apacheria-siglo-xlx-2/

https://www.archives.gov/research

https://www.arizonacivilwarcouncil.com/post/until-its-too-late

https://digitalcommos.trinity.edu/socanthro_honors/13

https://www.dignitymemorial.com/obituaries/corpus-christi-tx/reyes-castillo-8886194

https://www.dignitymemorial.com/obituaries/corpus-christi-tx/rosa-caballero-9979356

https://doi.org/10.1093/acrefore/9780199366439.013.21

https://doi.org/10.1215/00182168-43.1.34

https://en.wikipedia.org/w/index.php?title=Department_of_New_Mexico&oldid=1145042237

https://www.familysearch.org

https://www.familysearch.org/ark:/61903/1:1:QGMR-9NQR

https://www.forttours.com/pages/arroyobaluarte.asp

https://www.govinfo.gov/app/details/SERIALSET-00778_00_00-002-0001-0000/summary

https://historycollection.com/governments-used-to-pay-for-native-american-scalps-which-made-scalping-a-booming-business/

https://www.historynet.com/battle-cieneguilla-dragoons-vs-jicarilla-apaches/

https://www.historynet.com/victorios-war/

https://www.hmdb.org/m.asp?m=180612

http://www.jstor.org/stable/40167089

https://www.menardnews.com/news/more-things-change-4

https://www.nps.gov/articles/000/what-happened-to-the-bison.htm

https://www.nps.gov/parkhistory/online_books/amis/aspr-34/app4_files/sheet008.htm

https://obc.cclibraries.com/list/tv/van-buren-michael-e

https://www.okhistory.org/publications/enc/entry?entry=TW005

https://play.google.com/books/reader?

id=OQ1FAQAAMAAJ&pg=GBS.

PA28&printsec=frontcover&output=re

ader&hl=en&pg=GBS.PA29

https://portal.tamucc.edu/search/?

searchtype=o&searcharg=19135414

https://texashistory.unt.edu/ark:/67531/metapth1094930/m1/2/

https://texashistory.unt.edu/ark:/67531/metapth1095293/m1/2/

https://texashistory.unt.edu/ark:/67531/metapth81148/

https://www.tshaonline.org/handbook/entries/collins-tx-nueces-county

http://www.tshaonline.org/handbook/entries/los-presenos-tx

https://www.wikipedia.com

https://www.worldstatesmen.org/US_NativeAM.html

https://irp.fas.org/agency/army/short.pdf

AI Utilized

Google AI Overview 3/3/2025 "Were Lipan Teepees made of Canvas?"

Google AI Overview 3/3/2025 "Did Lipan use blankets?"

Google AI Overview 3/7/2025 "What would be the breakdown of a Native American group of 100?"

Google AI Overview 3/7/2025 "Mortality rate for Native Americans in 1850's

Index

www.ingramcontent.com/pod-product-compliance
Lightning Source LLC
Chambersburg PA
CBHW051204120626
46547CB00013B/1202